Building Blocks for the Development of an International Framework for the Governance of Space Resource Activities

AF182342

Building Blocks for the Development of an International Framework for the Governance of Space Resource Activities

A Commentary

Olavo De O. Bittencourt Neto, Mahulena Hofmann, Tanja Masson-Zwaan and Dimitra Stefoudi (Eds.)

eleven
international publishing

Published, sold and distributed by Eleven International Publishing
P.O. Box 85576
2508 CG The Hague
The Netherlands
Tel.: +31 70 33 070 33
Fax: +31 70 33 070 30
email: sales@elevenpub.nl
www.elevenpub.com

Sold and distributed in USA and Canada
Independent Publishers Group
814 N. Franklin Street
Chicago, IL 60610, USA
Order Placement: +1 800 888 4741
Fax: +1 312 337 5985
orders@ipgbook.com
www.ipgbook.com

Eleven International Publishing is an imprint of Boom uitgevers Den Haag.

ISBN 978-94-6236-121-8

© 2020 The authors | Eleven International Publishing

This publication is protected by international copyright law.
All rights reserved. No part of this publication may be reproduced, stored in a retrieval system, or transmitted in any form or by any means, electronic, mechanical, photocopying, recording or otherwise, without the prior permission of the publisher.

Printed in The Netherlands

Table of Contents

Introduction

The Hague International Space Resources Governance Working Group (Working Group) was established in 2015 with the objective to assess the need for a regulatory framework applicable to the use of mineral and volatile materials on the Moon and other celestial bodies, as well as to lay the groundwork for international deliberations on the potential development of such an international framework.

1 Mission

The Working Group was set up following the 'Roundtable on the Governance of Space Resources', convened by The Hague Institute for Global Justice on 1 December 2014. The event was attended by over 30 industry leaders, scientists, diplomats as well as political and legal experts from across the globe and it served as a forum to discuss and propose solutions for the current lack of a clear legal framework related to the use of space resources found on asteroids and other celestial bodies, including the Moon. The Working Group was then established to support this process and promote its advancement, within a reasonable time frame and in accordance with international law.[1]

Set to operate in a transparent and open manner, the Working Group promoted international cooperation and multi-stakeholder dialogue between members and observers representing governments, international organizations, academia, industry and other actors of the global civil society, including representatives of the United Nations Office of Outer Space Affairs (UNOOSA), toward the consideration of significant aspects related to space resource activities. Its mission was to offer a useful contribution to the international community on its subject matter, creating an enabling environment for space resource activities.

During its activities, the Working Group aimed first to assess, on a global scale, the need for a governing framework for space resource activities and, once that was settled, to prepare a document identifying the main applicable governance features. In order to achieve its goal, the Working Group promoted the identification and formulation of building blocks for the governance of space resource activities ('Building Blocks'), as well as recommendations on a possible implementation strategy.

The Building Blocks, commented herein, are designed to serve as the basis for a possible international framework, without prejudice to its form and structure. In its final form,

1 UN Doc. A/AC.105/C.2/2016/CRP.17.

twenty provisions, elaborated during the various meetings of the Working Group, were accepted and approved. The Building Blocks address general matters, such as the objective of an international legal framework, the definitions of key terms, and the scope and principles of an international legal framework, as well as substantive matters, including jurisdiction over space resource activities, access to and utilization of space resources, sharing of benefits arising out of the utilization of space resources, the exchange of information under the international legal framework, and liability, monitoring and compliance issues.

The principle of adaptive governance led the Working Group during the formulation of the Building Blocks, considering that space resource activities should be, in time, incrementally addressed, reflecting contemporary technology and practices. Thus, the natural evolution of governance mechanisms is properly embraced, coordinating effective solutions to inherent complex challenges, whenever realized.

Designed to foster synergy through dialogue, the Working Group considered the Building Blocks as its contribution to national, regional and global efforts on the governance of space resource activities.

2 Composition and Functioning of the Working Group

An international consortium was established to serve as the platform for the Working Group, involving partners representing organizations from all continents, and functioning under a Memorandum of Understanding. The founding consortium partner was the International Institute of Air and Space Law (IIASL) of Leiden University (the Netherlands), where the Working Group was hosted. The other consortium partners were: the Catholic University of Santos (UNISANTOS) (Brazil); the Centre for Resources, Energy and Environmental Law (CREEL) of the University of Melbourne (Australia); the Indonesian Centre for Air and Space Law (CASL) of Padjajaran University (Indonesia); the Secure World Foundation (SWF) (USA); the University of Cape Town (UCT) (South Africa), the University of Luxembourg (Luxembourg), the Nishimura Institute of Advanced Legal Studies (NIALS) (Japan), and the Ten to the Ninth Plus Foundation (USA).

The Working Group was serviced by a Secretariat, responsible for managing its operation and budget. It consisted of the Working Group's Executive Secretary (Giuseppe Reibaldi) and an Assistant Secretary (Merinda Stewart until September 2016, then Dimitra Stefoudi). The Working Group had a Chair (René Lefeber) and two Vice-Chairs (Michael Simpson and Olavo de O. Bittencourt Neto). Weekly calls were held between the Executive Secretary and the Assistant Secretary, in order to organize the activities of the Group and to progress its working plan. Coordination calls were also periodically arranged with the Chairs and the Vice-Chairs, to discuss critical issues and prepare for the face-to-face meetings. Additionally, according to the Memorandum of Understanding of the consortium, evaluation calls were held twice per year with the Executive and Assistant Secretary, in order to assess the progress of the work with the consortium partners. During the call, activities carried out by the partners and the execution of the MoU provisions in the past as well as in the future, were discussed.

The Working Group was composed of members and observers from government, industry, universities and research centers. They were responsible for making the decisions and were invited to attend all teleconferences and meetings of the Working Group. The number of members to the Working Group was finally limited to a total of 35, reflecting an ample and geographically inclusive composition. Additionally, professionals directly involved in space resources issues were welcomed as observers to face-to-face meetings. Except for location limits, there were no restrictions on the overall number of observers to the Working Group; however, the number of observers per organization was limited to one. A formal application to the Secretariat was required in order to become an observer, in accordance with a published procedure. The Secretariat decided on a case by case basis about the relevance of the application for the Working Group. The list of members and observers from 2016 to 2019 can be found in Annex I.

The Working Group was present, through its members and observers, at various international events in an effort to increase the transparency and outreach of its outreach activities. Moreover, the consortium partners organized several dedicated activities, promoting the Working Group and raising awareness on the issue of space resource governance. Those actions are listed in the final report of the first phase and the final report of the second phase, which can be found on the website of the Working Group.

A total of eight face-to-face meetings of the Working Group were convened between 2016 and 2019; other activities were conducted via email or teleconference calls.

3 Face-to-Face Meetings

The Working Group spread its activities over two phases, the first from 2016 to 2017, and the second from 2018 to 2019. In the first phase of its activities, the first face-to-face meeting of the Working Group was held from 18 to 19 April 2016 at Leiden University, the Netherlands. It was attended by a majority of members and a large number of observers. The meeting facilitated an extensive discussion on the proposed Building Blocks of the project, forming the basis for a possible international framework on space resource activities.

Later that year, from 7 to 8 November 2016, the second face-to-face meeting was held at Leiden University. The debates were based on the previously formulated draft Building Blocks, inviting participants to further elaborate on their content and realizing the main elements required for establishing an international framework.

Leiden University also hosted the third face-to-face meeting, from 10 to 12 April 2017. The participants continued to discuss the content of the draft Building Blocks and extensively addressed the various issues related to the governance of space resources. Also, outreach activities were considered and discussed.

The Working Group reconvened in Leiden for the fourth face-to-face meeting from 11 to 13 September 2017. After comprehensive deliberations, the meeting successfully concluded the first phase of the Working Group, consolidating the text of the draft Building Blocks into a set of general guidelines that would be made public and open for comments. However, the participants felt that the Working Group could continue to contribute to its subject matter by promoting further discussions on the draft Building Blocks. The recommendation of the members was to extend the operation of the Working Group for at least two more years, creating panels (technical and socio-economic) to support its activities, together with the suggestion to increase the number of stakeholders involved in the further consideration of the draft Building Blocks. Additionally, it was decided that the Working Group should incorporate henceforth the word 'international' in its title.

During the fourth face-to-face meeting, the Working Group agreed to circulate the text of the draft Building Blocks, acknowledging them as initial outcome of its work.[2] Accordingly, the document was made public and opened for comments for several months, including at the United Nations Committee for the Peaceful Uses of Outer Space, during a side event held during the fifty-seventh session of the Legal Subcommittee, on 13 April 2018, organized by the University of Vienna as Austrian 'National Point of Contact' of the European Centre for Space Law.

During the second phase of its work, the Working Group held four face-to-face meetings. The first occurred at Leiden University from 23 to 24 April 2018, further addressing the draft Building Blocks while acknowledging early international feedback. In that event, the Working Group approved a proposal to develop a specific document providing commentaries on the Building Blocks ('Commentary'), explaining and clarifying its provisions and providing details on alternatives that had been discussed, in order to be presented to the international community. It was agreed that the Commentary should specifically address the content of each Building Block, while reflecting on the respective debates and advancing the Working Group's mission.

The second face-to-face meeting of phase two took place at the University of Luxembourg, from 29 to 30 November 2018, with the majority of members and observers attending. At the event, comments received on the draft Building Blocks during the one-year public consultation period were thoroughly reviewed. Furthermore, the Technical Panel,

---

2 A booklet titled 'Draft Building Blocks for the Development of an International Framework on Space Resource Activities' was printed in 1500 copies and distributed all over the world, in order to spread the initial results of the Working Group and to facilitate the open consultation process.

chaired by Kyle Acierno, presented its report to the Working Group, consisting of input on issues related to frequency allocation for deep space missions, case studies on the definition of principles related to safety zones, as well as general technical remarks on selected Building Blocks. The Socio-Economic Panel, chaired by Ian Christensen, presented its work plan for the second phase, elaborating on the topics of societal and ethical aspects of space resource utilization, protection of the outer space environment, and financial prospects for the use of space resources.

The Working Group returned to Leiden University for the third face-to-face meeting of the second phase, which took place from 15 to 16 April 2019. Comments received following the meeting of November 2018 were examined, along with additional feedback formulated by members and observers. The Socio-Economic Panel reported to the Working Group regarding its work on key aspects of space resource utilization, including social licenses to operate, responsible investment, cooperation models and capacity building. The action plan, guidelines and draft format for the Commentary were presented, introducing the members of the Drafting Committee and resource persons participating in the effort. The Commentary's objectives and format were presented for approval.

The final fourth face-to-face meeting of the second phase was held at the University of Luxembourg from 11 to 13 November 2019. Concluding the mission of the Working Group, the Building Blocks were accorded in their final form and accepted for publication and distribution along with the Commentary.

4 Commentary

The Commentary was designed to clarify the content of each Building Block, reflecting agreed provisions and suggestions, as accorded by the Working Group, and to provide additional observations to illustrate their *raison d'être*. Additionally, this action was envisioned as an instrument to present the output of the Working Group to the general public, including information about its mission, composition, phases and procedure, while developing an additional channel of communication with the international community to foster the discussion on the Working Group topics.

As a collaborative effort, the Commentary was developed by a Drafting Committee composed of Olavo de O. Bittencourt Neto (Action Manager), Mahulena Hofmann, Tanja Masson-Zwaan, and Dimitra Stefoudi. Research assistance was provided by Thomas Cheney, Sara Ferreira, Dovilé Matuleviciute, Antonino Salmeri and Martin Svec.

The Drafting Committee was responsible for preparing early drafts of the Commentary, as well as consolidating the final text. In order to accomplish its mission, the Drafting Committee followed terms of reference approved by the Working Group, while securing consistency, structure and proper examination of its members' contributions.

All decisions of the Drafting Committee were made by consensus, through meetings and other forms of communication between its members.

The Building Blocks were commented in accordance with the following format:

1. Text of the Building Block;
2. Explanation of the Building Block, justifying its inclusion and reviewing its content;
3. Identification of applicable legal basis, considering primary sources of law; and
4. Acknowledgement of alternatives discussed during the meetings, identifying possible areas of disagreement.

The present document represents the final version of the Commentary, as concluded by the Drafting Committee and approved by the Secretariat. It is preceded by the full text of the Building Blocks. Additionally, the following documents are included, as annexes: list of consortium partners, members and observers of the Working Group (Annex I); Report of the Technical Panel (Annex II); and Report of the Socio-Economic Panel (Annex III).

Building Blocks

Building Blocks for the Development of an International Framework on Space Resource Activities

Introduction

The utilization of space resources has great potential for the future of humankind. In order to create an enabling environment for space resource activities, The Hague International Space Resources Governance Working Group was created to promote international cooperation and multi-stakeholder dialogue. It has designed the building blocks below to lay the groundwork for international discussions on the potential development of an international framework, without prejudice to its form and structure. The Working Group adopted the Building Blocks on 12 November 2019. Pending the adoption and the operationalization of the international framework, States, international organizations, and non-governmental entities are encouraged to consider and use the Building Blocks.

Guided by the principle of adaptive governance, the Working Group considered it neither necessary nor feasible to attempt to comprehensively address space resource activities in the building blocks: space resource activities should be incrementally addressed at the appropriate time on the basis of contemporary technology and practices.

A commentary on the development of the Building Blocks with information on each of the Building Blocks will be made available at the beginning of 2020. Information about its publication will be posted on the website of the Working Group.[1]

The Working Group hopes that its activities will complement other efforts at the national, regional and global level to address space resource activities.

1 Objective

1.1 The international framework should create an enabling environment for space resource activities that takes into account all interests and benefits all countries and humankind.
1.2 To achieve this objective, the international framework should:

1 https://www.universiteitleiden.nl/en/law/institute-of-public-law/institute-of-air-space-law/the-hague-space-resources-governance-working-group (accessed and verified on 20 December 2019).

a. Identify and define the relationship of space resource activities with existing international space law, including the provisions of the United Nations treaties on outer space;
b. Propose recommendations for the consideration of States for the application or development of domestic frameworks;
c. Propose recommendations for the consideration of international organizations for the application or development of internal frameworks;
d. Promote the identification of best practices by States, international organizations and non-governmental entities.

2 *Definition of key terms*

2.1 *Space resource*: an extractable and/or recoverable abiotic resource *in situ* in outer space;[2]
2.2 *Utilization of space resources*: the recovery of space resources and the extraction of raw mineral or volatile materials therefrom;[3]
2.3 *Space resource activity*: an activity conducted in outer space for the purpose of searching for space resources, the recovery of those resources and the extraction of raw mineral or volatile materials therefrom, including the construction and operation of associated extraction, recovery, processing and transportation systems;
2.4 *Space object*: an object launched into outer space from Earth, including component parts thereof as well as its launch vehicle and parts thereof;
2.5 *Space-made product*: a product made in outer space wholly or partially from space resources;[4]
2.6 *Operator*: a governmental, international or non-governmental entity conducting space resource activities.

3 *Scope*

3.1 The international framework should address States and international organizations, and could provide for the regulation of the conduct of States, international organizations, and non-governmental entities.

2 According to the understanding of the Working Group, this includes mineral and volatile materials, including water, but excludes (a) satellite orbits; (b) radio spectrum; and (c) energy from the sun except when collected from unique and scarce locations.

3 According to the understanding of the Working Group, this excludes secondary utilization of space resources, *i.e.* (a) utilization of raw materials derived from space resources; and (b) marketing and distribution of space resources.

4 According to the understanding of the Working Group, this excludes raw mineral and volatile materials, including water, irrespective of form.

3.2 The international framework should address space resource activities within the solar system.

4 *Principles*

4.1 The international framework should be consistent with international law.

4.2 The international framework should be designed to:

a. Adhere to the principle of adaptive governance by incrementally regulating space resource activities at the appropriate time;
b. Promote compatibility and predictability of domestic frameworks of States and internal frameworks of international organizations;
c. Contribute to sustainable development;
d. Prevent disputes arising out of space resource activities;
e. Promote and secure the orderly and safe utilization of space resources;
f. Promote the sustainable, rational, efficient and economic use of space resources;
g. Promote the use of sustainable technology;
h. Provide legal certainty and predictability for operators;
i. Take into particular account the needs of developing countries;
j. Take into particular account the needs of science;
k. Take into particular account the contributions of pioneer operators.

4.3 The international framework should provide that:

a. Space resources shall be used exclusively for peaceful purposes;
b. Space resource activities shall be carried out for the benefit and in the interests of all countries and humankind irrespective of their degree of economic and scientific development;
c. Appropriate international consultations shall be undertaken in accordance with Article IX OST[5] if there is a reason to believe that any potentially harmful interference may be caused;
d. International cooperation in space resource activities shall be conducted in accordance with international law.

---

5 1967 Treaty on Principles Governing the Activities of States in the Exploration and Use of Outer Space, including the Moon and Other Celestial Bodies.

5 *International responsibility for space resource activities*

The international framework should provide that:

a. States shall bear international responsibility for national space resource activities, whether such activities are carried out by governmental agencies or non-governmental entities, and for ensuring that such activities are carried out in conformity with the international framework;
b. Non-governmental space resource activities shall require prior authorization and continuing supervision by the appropriate State;
c. When space resource activities are carried out by an international organization, responsibility for compliance with the international framework shall be borne by the international organization and by the States participating in such organization.

6 *Jurisdiction and control over space-made products used in space resource activities*

The international framework should provide that States have jurisdiction and control over any space-made products used in the space resource activities for which they are responsible.

7 *Priority rights*

The international framework should enable the attribution of priority rights to an operator to search for and/or recover space resources for a maximum period of time and a maximum area upon registration in an international registry, and provide for the international recognition of such priority rights. The attribution, duration, and the area of the priority right should be determined on the basis of the specific circumstances of a proposed space resource activity.

8 *Resource rights*

8.1 The international framework should ensure that resource rights over raw mineral and volatile materials extracted from space resources, as well as products derived therefrom, can lawfully be acquired through domestic legislation, bilateral agreements and/or multilateral agreements.

8.2 The international framework should enable the mutual recognition between States of such resource rights.

8.3 The international framework should ensure that the utilization of space resources is carried out in accordance with the principle of non-appropriation under Article II OST.

9 *Due regard for corresponding interests of all countries and humankind*

The international framework should provide that States and international organizations responsible for space resource activities shall give due regard to the corresponding interests of all countries and humankind.

10 *Avoidance and mitigation of potentially harmful impacts resulting from space resource activities*

Taking into account the current state of technology, the international framework should provide that States and international organizations responsible for space resource activities shall adopt appropriate measures with the aim of avoiding and mitigating potentially harmful impacts, including:

a. Risks to the safety of persons, the environment or property;
b. Damage to persons, the environment or property;
c. Adverse changes in the environment of the Earth, taking into account internationally agreed planetary protection policies;
d. Harmful contamination of celestial bodies, taking into account internationally agreed planetary protection policies;
e. Harmful contamination of outer space;
f. Harmful effects of the creation of space debris;
g. Harmful interference with other on-going space activities, including other space resource activities;
h. Changes to designated and internationally endorsed outer space natural or cultural heritage sites;
i. Adverse changes to designated and internationally endorsed outer space sites of scientific interest.

11 *Technical standards for, prior review of, and safety zones around space resource activities*

11.1 The international framework should provide that States and international organizations shall require the conduct of a review prior to a decision to proceed with a space resource activity to ascertain that such an activity is carried out in a safe manner to avoid harmful impacts.

11.2 The international framework should encourage the development of:

a. Procedures to ensure that equipment, operational procedures, and processes applied in space resource activities avoid harmful impacts;

b. Methodologies to assess that equipment, operational procedures, and processes applied in space resource activities meet common technical standards (conformity assessment);
c. Technical standards for equipment, operational procedures, and processes applied in space resource activities (standardization).

11.3 Taking into account the principle of non-appropriation under Article II OST, the international framework should permit States and international organizations responsible for space resource activities to establish a safety zone, or other area-based safety measure, around an area identified for a space resource activity as necessary to assure safety and to avoid any harmful interference with that space resource activity. Such safety measure shall not impede the free access, in accordance with international law, to any area of outer space by personnel, vehicles and equipment of another operator. In accordance with the area-based safety measure, a State or international organization may restrict access for a limited period of time, provided that timely public notice has been given setting out the reasons for such restriction.

11.4 The international framework should provide that appropriate international consultations are undertaken in case of possible overlap of safety zones or conflicts involving the freedom of access recognized by international law.

12 Monitoring and redressing harmful impacts resulting from space resource activities

12.1 The international framework should provide that States and international organizations shall ensure monitoring of any harmful impacts resulting from space resource activities for which they are responsible.

12.2 If a harmful impact resulting from a space resource activity occurs, or is reasonably expected to occur, the international framework should provide that the State or international organization responsible for the space resource activity shall implement measures to respond to such harmful impact (response measures) and consider whether the space resource activity should be adjusted or terminated (adaptive management).

13 Sharing of benefits arising out of the utilization of space resources

13.1 Bearing in mind that the exploration and use of outer space shall be carried out for the benefit and in the interests of all countries and humankind, the international framework should provide that States and international organizations responsible for space resource activities shall provide for benefit-sharing through the promotion of the participation in space resource activities by all countries, in particular developing countries. Benefits may include, but not be limited to, enabling, facilitating, promoting, and fostering:

a. The development of space science and technology and of its applications;
b. The development of relevant and appropriate capabilities in interested States;
c. Cooperation and contribution in education and training;
d. Access to and exchange of information;
e. Incentivization of joint ventures;
f. The exchange of expertise and technology among States on a mutually acceptable basis;
g. The establishment of an international fund.

13.2 The international framework should not require compulsory monetary benefit-sharing.

13.3 Operators should be encouraged to provide for benefit-sharing.

14 *Registration and sharing of information*

The international framework should provide that States and international organizations shall:

a. Register priority rights of an operator to search and/or recover space resources in accordance with the international framework;
b. Give advance notification of space resource activities, including any area-based safety measure associated with them, for which they are responsible through an international database;
c. Register space objects in accordance with the REG,[6] United Nations General Assembly Resolution 1721 B (XVI),[7] or Article XI OST, taking into account United Nations General Assembly Resolution 62/101;[8]
d. Notify frequency assignments for recording in the Master International Frequency Register in accordance with the Radio Regulations of the International Telecommunication Union;
e. Provide, taking into account Article XI OST and the legitimate interests of operators, information and best practices on the prior authorization and continuing supervision of space resource activities for which they are responsible through an international database, including:
    i. The purposes, locations, orbital parameters, and duration of space resource activities;
    ii. The nature, conduct, and locations of space resource activities and associated logistic activities, for example deployment of stations, installations, equipment and vehicles;
    iii. The results of space resource activities;

6 1975 Convention on the Registration of Objects Launched into Outer Space.

7 1961 Resolution 1721 B (XVI) adopted by the United Nations General Assembly, International Cooperation on the Peaceful Uses of Outer Space.

8 2007 Resolution 62/101 adopted by the United Nations General Assembly, Recommendations on enhancing the practice of States and international intergovernmental organizations in registering space objects.

iv. Any phenomena discovered in outer space which could endanger terrestrial life or health, as well as of any indication of extraterrestrial life;
v. Any harmful impacts resulting from space resource activities for which they are responsible and the measures planned or implemented to redress such impacts;

f. Notify the termination of space resource activities for which they are responsible through an international database together with a statement on the condition of the area where the space resource activity was carried out, including the presence of any space objects or space-made products, or parts thereof.

15 *Provision of assistance in case of distress*

The international framework should provide for the applicability of Article V OST and the ARRA[9] to persons involved in space resource activities.

16 *Liability in case of damage resulting from space resource activities*

16.1 The international framework should provide for the applicability of Articles VI and VII OST and the LIAB[10] to damage resulting from space resource activities.
16.2 The international framework should encourage initiatives of operators to provide, individually or collectively, compensation for damage resulting from their space resource activities.

17 *Visits relating to space resource activities*

The international framework should provide for the applicability of Article XII OST, taking into account the legitimate interests of operators, including safety of operations and protection of intellectual property.

18 *Institutional arrangements*

The international framework should provide for:

a. The establishment and maintenance of a publicly available international registry for registering priority rights of an operator to search and/or recover space resources;

---

9 1968 Agreement on the Rescue of Astronauts, the Return of Astronauts and the Return of Objects Launched into Space.
10 1972 Convention on International Liability for Damage Caused by Space Objects.

b. The establishment and maintenance of an international database, in addition to the international registry, for making publicly available:
   i. Advance notifications of space resource activities, including any area-based safety measures;
   ii. Information and best practices;
   iii. The list of designated and internationally endorsed outer space natural and cultural heritage sites; and
   iv. The list of designated and internationally endorsed sites of scientific interest;
   v. Information and best practices on the prior authorization and continuing supervision of space resource activities for which States and international organizations are responsible;
   vi. Notifications of the termination of space resource activities for which States and international organizations are responsible.
c. The designation or establishment of an international body or bodies responsible for:
   i. The consideration and promotion of best practices;
   ii. The listing of designated and internationally endorsed outer space natural and cultural heritage sites, and sites of scientific interest;
   iii. The monitoring and review of the implementation of the international framework; and
   iv. The governance of the international registry, the international database and any other mechanism that may be established for the implementation of the international framework.

19 Settlement of disputes

The international framework should encourage recourse by States, international organizations and operators to the resolution of disputes through adjudicatory, non-adjudicatory or hybrid mechanisms, for example by developing procedures for consultation or promoting the use of the 2011 Permanent Court of Arbitration Optional Rules for Arbitration of Disputes Relating to Outer Space Activities.

20 Monitoring and review

Mechanisms should be developed for monitoring implementation of the international framework, for example on the basis of reports of States and international organizations, as well as for its review and further development consistent with the principle of adaptive governance.

Commentary

1 Objective

1 *Text*

1.1 The international framework should create an enabling environment for space resource activities that takes into account all interests and benefits all countries and humankind.

1.2 To achieve this objective, the international framework should:

a. **Identify and define the relationship of space resource activities with existing international space law, including the provisions of the United Nations treaties on outer space;**
b. **Propose recommendations for the consideration of States for the application or development of domestic frameworks;**
c. **Propose recommendations for the consideration of international organizations for the application or development of internal frameworks;**
d. **Promote the identification of best practices by States, international organizations and non-governmental entities.**

2 *Explanation*

The first Building Block identifies the main objective to be pursued by the international framework applicable to space resource activities, *i.e.*, to develop an enabling environment while considering general interest and benefits of all countries and humankind (paragraph 1), as well as initiatives designed to achieve such a goal (paragraph 2).

Space resource activities are considered as requiring a proper framework, capable of identifying and promoting desirable conducts from the relevant actors. At the same time, by recognizing the different perspectives *vis-à-vis* space resource activities, referring not only to countries, but also to humankind as a whole, Building Block 1 illustrates the inclusiveness, instrumental for attaining international legitimacy, which permeates the entire document.

An enabling environment, as mentioned in paragraph 1, is to be understood as including a set of rules, regulations, procedures and/or conditions capable of producing optimal results, as far as space resource activities are concerned, while minimizing and managing risks, in accordance with a comprehensive and inclusive outlook. In this regard, an enabling environment relies upon the consideration of different perspectives emerging from the actors involved in space resource activities, as well as the interests and benefits of all countries and humankind.

Such a goal requires specific measures, to be conveniently contemplated, as covered by paragraph 2. Indeed, the rapport between space resource activities and the space law instruments and rules, composing the '*corpus iuris spatialis*', is to be understood, in all its nuances, so as to identify the applicable legal principles and ensure compliance therewith. In accordance with subparagraph (a), particular attention should be devoted to the treaties on outer space concluded under the auspices of the United Nations, which are: the Outer Space Treaty (OST), of 1967;[1] the Rescue Agreement (ARRA), of 1968;[2] the Liability Convention (LIAB), of 1972;[3] the Registration Convention (REG), of 1975;[4] and the Moon Agreement (MA), of 1979.[5]

Subparagraph (b) indicates that the international framework should be pro-active, by proposing recommendations for States for the application or development of domestic frameworks. Guidance could also be offered to international organizations, in relation to their internal frameworks, as specified in subparagraph (c). The development or application of national governance regulations, in parallel with or in anticipation of an international framework, is thus acknowledged by Building Block 1, which considers overall consistency of fundamental importance for achieving the objective set forth in the first paragraph.

Subparagraph (d) encourages best practices related to space resource activities to be identified, whether emanating from States, international organizations or non-governmental organizations. For the purposes of this document, best practices are understood as commercial or professional procedures accepted or prescribed as capable of producing optimal results in relation to its subject matter, in accordance with practice and research, therefore serving as standards and lessons suitable for comprehensive consideration. Therefore, the use of the term in Building Block 1 is not intended to imply that certain practices are deemed better than others, but rather to indicate procedures to be properly appraised from the perspective of States and international organizations, especially those with experience or active presence in the field.

---

1 Treaty on Principles Governing the Activities of States in the Exploration and Use of Outer Space, including the Moon and Other Celestial Bodies, 610 UNTS 205, 1967. Status in 2019: 109 ratifications, 23 signatures.

2 Agreement on the Rescue of Astronauts, the Return of Astronauts and the Return of Objects Launched into Space, 672 UNTS 11, 1968. Status in 2019: 98 ratifications, 23 signatures, 3 declaration of acceptance of rights and obligations.

3 Convention on International Liability for Damage Caused by Space Objects, 961 UNTS 187, 1972. Status in 2019: 96 ratifications, 19 signatures, 4 declaration of acceptance of rights and obligations.

4 Convention on Registration of Objects Launched into Outer Space, 1023 UNTS 15. Status in 2019: 69 ratifications, 3 signatures, 4 declaration of acceptance of rights and obligations.

5 Agreement Governing the Activities of States on the Moon and Other Celestial Bodies, 1363 UNTS 3. Status in 2019: 18 ratifications, 4 signatures.

Hence, Building Block 1.2 addresses governance on different levels, both national and international, aiming to encompass the interests of all potential actors involved in space resource activities, namely States and private entities under their jurisdiction, international organizations and non-governmental organizations. The recommendations are not to be considered in any way as exhaustive, but rather as an indication of concerns or ideas deemed significant by the Working Group. Given that space law is dedicated to the governance of the activities of States in outer space and that some of the central discussion points regarding space resource activities are connected to their legality, the UN space treaties can function as initial point of consideration when it comes to the objectives of the international framework, irrespective of other relevant sources of law.

The objective set forth by Building Block 1 of creating an enabling environment for space resource activities, as well as the suggestions designed to achieve it, refer to a potential future international framework to be negotiated and established by the subjects of international law, *i.e.* States and international organizations. Since the purpose of the Building Blocks is to lay the groundwork for the introduction of such framework, the subsequent provisions include wide-ranging suggestions related to space resource activities and its actors.

The term 'international framework' has been chosen by the Working Group for its openness, and particularly for the fact that it neither defines the legal value of the Building Blocks, nor envisages the outcome of the activities of the UNCOPUOS in this area.

3 Legal Basis

The interest of all countries, irrespective of their degree of economic or scientific development, regarding the exploration and use of outer space, is acknowledged by Article I OST, in its first paragraph:

> The exploration and use of outer space, including the Moon and other celestial bodies, shall be carried out for the benefit and in the interests of all countries, irrespective of their degree of economic or scientific development, and shall be the province of all mankind.

For the States Parties to the MA, there is similar is the wording in its Article 4, which in paragraph 1 reads:

> The exploration and use of the Moon shall be the province of all mankind and shall be carried out for the benefit and in the interests of all countries, irrespective of their degree of economic or scientific development.

Such a principle was originally recognized in paragraph 1 of the United Nations General Assembly 'Declaration of Legal Principles Governing the Acts of States in the Exploration and Use of Outer Space' (Declaration of Legal Principles), of 1963,[6] as follows:

> The exploration and use of outer space shall be carried on for the benefit and in the interests of all mankind.

In 1996, through the 'Declaration on International Cooperation in the Exploration and Use of Outer Space for the Benefit and in the Interest of All States, Taking into Particular Account the Needs of Developing Countries',[7] the United Nations General Assembly reiterated the wide ranging orientation toward space activities, and included, in paragraph 1, particular reference to the needs of developing countries:

> International cooperation in the exploration and use of outer space for peaceful purposes (hereafter 'international cooperation') shall be conducted in accordance with the provisions of international law, including the Charter of the United Nations and the Treaty on the Principles Governing the Activities of States in the Exploration and Use of Outer Space, including the Moon and Other Celestial Bodies. It shall be carried out for the benefit and in the interest of all States, irrespective of their degree of economic, social or scientific and technological development, and shall be the province of all mankind. Particular account should be taken of the needs of developing countries.

4 *Alternatives Discussed*

Building Block 1 was introduced for open discussion at the Working Group during its first face-to-face meeting, in April 2016. Originally, it was composed only of the segment currently covered by paragraph 1. Only later, during the face-to-face meeting of April 2017, members and observers agreed that an additional paragraph should be created to describe and clarify the intentions of the Building Block and include the general consideration provisions as a new paragraph 2.

The content of the Building Block was not regarded as particularly contentious. Debate revolved around clarifying and improving the language used, and as a result the final version does not differ much from the original starting point.

6 UN Res. 1962 (XVIII), 13 December 1963.

7 UN Res. 51/122, 13 December 1996.

Concerning paragraph 1, it was discussed whether the expression 'international framework' was the most appropriate. In the end, the members and observers concluded that this formulation was broad enough and that the final form of the text would be decided at a later stage by the appropriate forum.

Additionally, the Working Group deliberated which interests should be taken into account when drafting the international framework. The first version of the Building Block mentioned 'public and commercial' interests, but with the progression of the debate and discussion, members and observers were of the opinion that 'public and private' would be more appropriate, allowing to also incorporate scientific interests, which could be either public or private and also not merely commercial. In the end, the members and observers reached consensus on the term 'all interests', since the focus was not actually public or private, but the benefit of all, considering the expression broad enough to convey that idea. However, some members and observers expressed their concern of possible overreaching in that regard.

The expression 'humankind' was added after the April 2017 meeting as the agreed gender-neutral version of the similar expression used in the UN treaties on outer space, 'mankind'. With this, the wording of the Building Block followed as close as possible the expressions used in the UN treaties. This is also the main reason why 'countries' was used instead of, for example, States. Additionally, members and observers were of the opinion that 'countries' was a more geographically representative term. The possibility of adding a reference to present and future generations was also discussed.

Some members and observers suggested to add reference to 'cooperation' in this paragraph, but ultimately it was decided that even though the term is often found in the UN treaties on outer space, it should not be included here.

Paragraph 2, subparagraph (a) was introduced after the meeting of April 2016, because members and observers were of the opinion that the relationship of space resource activities with existing international space law should be properly acknowledged by the international framework. Originally, the provision mentioned that the international framework should 'clarify' the relationship to 'existing provisions of United Nations treaties on outer space'. However, members and observers perfected the language of the provision, and concluded that 'identify and define' would be better, since clarity is needed in order to decide on binding and/or non-binding provisions for this relationship. Additionally, the expression 'international space law' was used, so as not to restrict the provision to the UN treaties on outer space. The issue of whether all UN treaties on outer space should be considered or merely those more widely ratified and accepted was also raised, but ultimately the wording of the provision remained as it is.

With regard to subparagraph (b), the original starting point of the provision mentioned 'guidance for the development of national frameworks' and not recommendations. However, members and observers later shared the opinion that the wording should be changed into 'propose recommendations', since the purpose of the Working Group is not to develop a draft instrument, but to provide suggestions in the format of Building Blocks In the face-to-face meeting of November 2016, a reference was added to international intergovernmental organizations, which was later changed to international organizations since members and observers considered the broader expression more appropriate. This reference evolved into subparagraph (c) after the meeting of September 2017.

With regard to subparagraph (d), the original version mentioned only States, following the example of Article VI OST. However, after the September 2017 meeting, the Working Group decided to broaden the provision, considering particularly international organizations, non-governmental organizations and private industry. Concerns were raised as to the use of the expression 'best practices'; it was even suggested to use only the word 'practice', since the Working Group did not intend to put the practice of one State above another. However, it was ultimately concluded that 'best practices' is a term of art referring to general standards, not customary law, and one which would be useful for space resource activities, particularly considering the expected major role of private industry.

2 Definition of Key Terms

1 Text

2.1 *Space resource*: an extractable and/or recoverable abiotic resource in situ in outer space;(i)
2.2 *Utilization of space resources*: the recovery of space resources and the extraction of raw mineral or volatile materials therefrom;(ii)
2.3 *Space resource activity*: an activity conducted in outer space for the purpose of searching for space resources, the recovery of those resources and the extraction of raw mineral or volatile materials therefrom, including the construction and operation of associated extraction, recovery, processing and transportation systems;
2.4 *Space object*: an object launched into outer space from Earth, including component parts thereof as well as its launch vehicle and parts thereof;
2.5 *Space-made product*: a product made in outer space wholly or partially from space resources;(iii)
2.6 *Operator*: a governmental, international or non-governmental entity conducting space resource activities.

(i) According to the understanding of the Working Group, this includes mineral and volatile materials, including water, but excludes (a) satellite orbits; (b) radio spectrum; and (c) energy from the sun except when collected from unique and scarce locations.

(ii) According to the understanding of the Working Group, this excludes secondary utilization of space resources, *i.e.* (a) utilization of raw materials derived from space resources; and (b) marketing and distribution of space resources.
(iii) According to the understanding of the Working Group, this excludes raw mineral and volatile materials, including water, irrespective of form.

2 *Explanation*

A total of six key terms, considered instrumental for the development of an international framework on space resource activities, are defined in Building Block 2. In separate paragraphs, it covered: (1) space resource, (2) utilization of space resources, (3) space resource activities, (4) space object, (5) space-made product and (6) operator. Additionally, four footnotes are included, to clarify and provide insight in relation to the content of respective definitions.

'Space resource' is the first term addressed, demonstrating its importance. In accordance with paragraph 2.1 and its footnote, a 'space resource' is first and foremost abiotic, understood as devoid of life, and found in outer space as its original place. Consequently, living natural resources eventually found or existent in celestial bodies are not covered by the Building Blocks. In order to be understood as such, a space resource must be capable of being extracted and/or recovered from its source. The definition lays its focus, therefore, on resources that can be obtained from celestial bodies, irrespective of the means of attainment.

In a footnote, the Working Group explains that the definition of space resource includes mineral and volatile materials, such as water, irrespective of their natural state. To provide further clarification, it is stated that satellite orbits, radio spectrum as well as energy from the sun, except when collected from unique and scarce locations, are excluded from the definition. Among such prime positions are the so-called 'peaks of eternal light', which refers to places on the surface of a celestial body where sunlight is almost continuously present.[8] Outer space sites of scientific interest are further considered in Building Block 10 regarding avoidance and mitigation of potentially harmful impacts resulting from space resource activities, and in Building Block 18 on institutional arrangements. As satellite orbits and radio spectrum are neither extractable nor recoverable, they are explicitly excluded from the definition. In addition, an international framework for use of satellite orbits and radio spectrum already exists in the instruments of the International Telecommunication Union.

8 Peaks of eternal light are highland regions, located e.g. near the lunar poles, continuously receiving sun light and, therefore, capable of providing permanent source of power.

The second key term defined is 'utilization of space resources', described in paragraph 2.2 as meaning the recovery of space resources, as well as the extraction of raw mineral and volatile material therefrom. space resources can be used for scientific purposes in addition to commercial and marketing purposes. Secondary utilization of space resources is nevertheless understood as being excluded from this definition, as stated in a footnote. Both the utilization of raw materials derived from space resources and the marketing and distribution of space resources are understood as secondary utilization. This exclusion was adopted by the Working Group, following the principle of adaptive governance, in order to establish a necessary cut-off point for applicability, considering the Building Blocks' characteristics.

Next, 'space resource activity' is addressed in paragraph 2.3 as an activity conducted in outer space for searching and recovery of space resources, as well as the extraction of raw mineral or volatile material therefrom. The concept includes the construction and operation of associated extraction, recovery, processing and transportation systems.

Concerning the specific wording used in this definition, 'searching for space objects' is a wide-ranging concept encompassing activities that are not necessarily conducted in outer space, such as, e.g., the use of telescopes from Earth to identify the features of a particular asteroid. Additionally, the terminology 'extraction, recovery, processing and transportation' was adopted so as not to exclude any relevant steps or phases of the applicable space resource activity, such as, or instance, sampling.

The definition of 'space object' is defined in paragraph 2.4 as any object launched into outer space from the Earth, therefore not covering launches from any other celestial body. In accordance with the definition provided by LIAB and REG, space objects include component parts thereof as well as their launch vehicle and parts thereof. Accordingly, objects not launched into outer space, like those created by 3D printing, fall outside the scope of paragraph 2.4.

A 'space-made product' is defined in paragraph 2.5 as one made, in whole or in part, from space resources, in outer space. A footnote was included to clarify that, in the opinion of the Working Group, raw mineral volatile materials, such as water, irrespective of form, are not covered by the definition of space-made product. The definition is also not applicable to any space debris resulting from, or related to, space objects.

Finally, paragraph 2.6 defines 'operator' as a governmental, international or non-governmental entity conducting space resource activities, therefore establishing a link with paragraph 2.3. This definition does not preclude natural persons to be considered as 'operators'.

3 *Legal Basis*

In order to elaborate Building Block 2, the Working Group took into consideration a number of regimes, from terrestrial mining to the Law of the Sea, as well as definitions incorporated by domestic space legislation in effect. Although the text does not follow a unique legal basis, the term 'space object' is defined in accordance with Article I, d LIAB and Article I, b REG:

> The term 'space object' includes component parts of a space object as well as its launch vehicle and parts thereof.

4 *Alternatives Discussed*

Throughout the drafting process, several terms were considered by the Working Group, which finally decided on those included in Building Block 2. Their respective definitions are envisioned as useful tools for proper understanding of the final document. The Working Group did not intend to explain all concepts applicable to the international framework. Nonetheless, several other Building Blocks detailed further concepts such as 'priority rights' (Building Block 7) and 'safety zones' (Building Block 11).

Among the terms considered by the Working Group but ultimately not included in Building Block 2, were 'celestial body', 'asteroid resource', 'geostationary' or 'harmful contamination'. In general, those terms were omitted due to lack of consensus or for not being indispensable in the context of space resource activities.

Regarding the definition of 'space resource', the original draft in the first face-to-face meeting in April 2016 did not include the notion of 'recoverable' and excluded only orbital positions and frequencies. The term 'abiotic' was preferred over 'non-living' as the latter would imply something that might have been previously alive. The term 'recoverable' also raised the question of sovereignty implications, 'extractable' being considered as a substitute, but finally both expressions were jointly used in paragraph 2.1. Recoverability was added to the definition, alongside extractability, in order to account for some resources being eventually harvested or collected from a surface and not exactly extracted therefrom, in view of evolving technology.

By the next face-to-face meeting, all the clarifications included as footnotes were incorporated, except for the situation involving energy collected from unique and scarce locations, which members and observers continued to discuss up until the April 2019 meeting. Other proposals contemplated the definition of terms such as 'man-made space object' and 'natural celestial bodies'.

Regarding the definition of 'utilization of space resources', the original draft, like many Building Blocks, while focusing on commercial purposes, already excluded secondary utilization of space resources. However, the Working Group rapidly reached consensus that this key term should not be limited to commercial purposes, but applies also to scientists, governments and non-governmental organizations. The issue and link with the recognition of property rights was also raised by several members and observers.

In relation to 'space resource activity', members and observers debated several different definitions, carefully following OST terminology. Terms such as 'exploitation', 'harvesting', 'prospecting', 'exploration' and 'use' were discussed, in accordance with a comparative approach applied to different legal areas, such as the law of the sea. In order to draft this definition, the Working Group took into consideration the six stages of the terrestrial mining industry, *i.e.* consultation, exploration, evaluation, development, production and closure. It was also discussed whether this definition should exclusively encompass commercial purposes, but members and observers ultimately decided otherwise. It was suggested to limit its scope to activities directly related to the search for and extraction of ore, but this idea was not adopted by the Working Group.

As far as the definition of 'space object' is concerned, the main discussion revolved around possible exclusion of objects made from space resources. Some members and observers argued in favour of taking the opportunity to proactively broaden the definition of the LIAB and REG. Based on concerns regarding possible liability issues resulting from space resource activities, some members and observers were of the opinion that the definition should be expanded, although the discussion mostly concerned the introduction of another key term, 'space-made product', which was not present in the first draft of the Building Blocks.

Regarding the definition of 'operator', considering the broadness of linking it to space resource activities conducted by 'governmental, international or non-governmental entity', a suggestion was made to use the word 'entity', but the former term was ultimately maintained by the Working Group for the sake of clarity and precision.

Minor modifications to the wording of Building Block 2 were agreed during the final session of November 2019.

3 Scope

1 Text

3.1 The international framework should address States and international organizations, and could provide for the regulation of the conduct of States, international organizations, and non-governmental entities.

3.2 The international framework should address space resource activities within the solar system.

2 *Explanation*

The personal scope of the international framework on space resource activities is addressed in Building Block 3, identifying which entities should enjoy rights and obligations. States, as the main subjects of international law, are specifically mentioned in paragraph 3.1, alongside international organizations, which also have international legal personality.

International instruments ultimately incorporating the building blocks cannot apply directly to natural persons, private entrepreneurs, private companies, as they are not subjects of public international law. Therefore, States should ensure that applicable procedures apply to these stakeholders, and the international framework can serve as basis or best practices for these entities. Non-governmental entities require authorization by States, in accordance with Article VI OST.

In accordance with international law, States are entities consisting of a territory and a population subjected to an organized political authority. States are sovereign, within the limits established by international law. On the other hand, international organizations are intergovernmental entities, created by States to perform specific functions with the purpose of achieving the common goals of their members.

Paragraph 3.1 clarifies that the international framework could regulate the conduct of not only States and international organizations, but also of non-governmental entities, *i.e.* those not affiliated to a State or local government through ownership or control. Alignment with Building Block 1, paragraph 1.2 (d) is therefore ensued. Consequently, the range of application envisioned by the Building Block is wide and comprehensive, in order to adapt the international framework to possible future developments in space resource activities.

As far as the territorial scope is concerned, paragraph 3.2 establishes that the international framework on space resource activities should be limited to those undertaken in or on celestial bodies located in the solar system, providing a clear *ratione loci* limitation towards outer space. The solar system is considered as the sun and those celestial bodies held by its attraction and revolving around it, including planets, asteroids and comets.

With regard to the temporal scope, the Working Group did not ignore that the international framework should have a time frame. However, in accordance with the principle of adaptive governance, it was agreed that such delimitation would not need to be covered by Building Block 3, since the nature of the international framework on space resource activities was not established.

3 Legal Basis

Support for the personal scope envisioned by Building Block 3 can be found in the OST. In accordance with its Article VI, States shall bear international responsibility for all national space activities, whether governmental or non-governmental. As far as international organizations are concerned, whenever carrying out space activities, responsibility shall be borne by both the international organizations and their States Parties. The text states:

> States Parties to the Treaty shall bear international responsibility for national activities in outer space, including the Moon and other celestial bodies, whether such activities are carried on by governmental agencies or by non-governmental entities, and for assuring that national activities are carried out in conformity with the provisions set forth in the present Treaty. The activities of non-governmental entities in outer space, including the Moon and other celestial bodies, shall require authorization and continuing supervision by the appropriate State Party to the Treaty. When activities are carried on in outer space, including the Moon and other celestial bodies, by an international organization, responsibility for compliance with this Treaty shall be borne both by the international organization and by the States Parties to the Treaty participating in such organization.

For the States Parties to the MA, said treaty provides for the same regime of State responsibility for national activities, reading in paragraph 1 of Article 14:

> States Parties to this Agreement shall bear international responsibility for national activities on the Moon, whether such activities are carried out by governmental agencies or by non-governmental entities, and for assuring that national activities are carried out in conformity with the provisions set forth in this Agreement. States Parties shall ensure that non-governmental entities under their jurisdiction shall engage in activities on the Moon only under the authority and continuing supervision of the appropriate State Party

Additionally, for the States Parties to the MA, the application of its provisions to the activities of international intergovernmental organizations is extended by virtue of Article 16, according to which:

> (...) References in this Agreement to States shall be deemed to apply to any international intergovernmental organization which conducts space activities if the organization declares its acceptance of the rights and obligations provided

> for in this Agreement and if a majority of the States members of the organization are States Parties to this Agreement and to the Treaty on Principles Governing the Activities of States in the Exploration and Use of Outer Space, including the Moon and Other Celestial Bodies. States members of any such organization which are States Parties to this Agreement shall take all appropriate steps to ensure that the organization makes a declaration in accordance with the foregoing.

The aforementioned provisions of the OST and the MA follow Principle 5 Declaration of Legal Principles, which provides:

> States bear international responsibility for national activities in outer space, whether carried on by governmental agencies or by non-governmental entities, and for assuring that national activities are carried on in conformity with the principles set forth in the present Declaration. The activities of non-governmental entities in outer space shall require authorization and continuing supervision by the State concerned. When activities are carried on in outer space by an international organization, responsibility for compliance with the principles set forth in this Declaration shall be borne by the international organization and by the States participating in it.

Regarding paragraph 3.2, its wording stems from Article 1, paragraph 1 MA:

> The provisions of this Agreement relating to the Moon shall also apply to other celestial bodies within the solar system, other than the Earth, except insofar as specific legal norms enter into force with respect to any of these celestial bodies.

4 Alternatives Discussed

Building Block 3 originally followed a different structure, aiming to cover subjective, functional and territorial scope. However, considering that the functional scope was essentially space resource activities, previously defined in Building Block 2, that provision was eventually excluded from the text.

Members and observers discussed whether the international framework should apply to non-governmental entities, particularly industry and individuals. The opinion was presented that the international framework could be more useful if that was the case, and examples such as jurisdiction of the Permanent Court of Arbitration and International Criminal Court were raised. A proposal was also made to include national activities authorized and/or supervised by States, following Article VI OST. Additionally, in Building Block 3 the term 'State' is used, contrary to 'country' found in other provisions. The WG found that even though the wording is not consistent, it was comfortable with its use, since it is in accordance with the UN outer space treaties. Finally, the Working Group accorded, in paragraph 3.1, that the international framework should address only States and international organizations, although the conduct of international organizations and non-governmental entities could be regulated.

Regarding the territorial scope, the original draft was based on Article 1, paragraph 1 MA, therefore including reference to celestial bodies. However, members and observers removed this mention, because to complications due to the absence of a valid and scientifically accurate definition of celestial bodies. A discussion was also held as to whether paragraph 3.2 should specifically exclude the Earth, with some members and observers having sustained that position, while others proposed to use the term 'space' or 'outer space' so as to include asteroids not part of the solar system and eventually passing through it. The Working Group in the end came to the conclusion that the territorial scope should be limited to the solar system, encompassing space resource activities therein.

Additionally, it was supported by some members and observers to include a provision mentioning the International Telecommunication Union (ITU), stating that the international framework should consider and complement its role in relation to radio spectrum and satellite orbits. The Technical Panel formed a team to consider the topic 'Coordinating use of the Radio Frequency and associated orbit for Missions to and on Celestial Bodies (Deep Space Missions)', which reviewed ITU regulations and considered, as its prime objective, to establish an initial pathway from research allocations to commercial allocations, recognizing that the radio frequencies to be used in lunar orbits should be available for commercial as well as scientific purposes, in order to provide certainty to all stakeholders. Considering that the Radio Regulations which regulate the use of radio frequencies and associated orbital positions, including those required for space resource activities, are updated by the World Radio Conference (WRC) of the ITU normally every four years, it was considered essential to study requirements of radio frequencies and associated orbital positions for space resource activities in a timely manner, as well as to convey them to appropriate WRCs for consideration. The final report of this panel is included as Annex II.

4 PRINCIPLES

1 Text

4.1 The international framework should be consistent with international law.

4.2 The international framework should be designed to:

a. **Adhere to the principle of adaptive governance by incrementally regulating space resource activities at the appropriate time;**
b. **Promote compatibility and predictability of domestic frameworks of States and internal frameworks of international organizations;**
c. **Contribute to sustainable development;**
d. **Prevent disputes arising out of space resource activities;**
e. **Promote and secure the orderly and safe utilization of space resources;**
f. **Promote the sustainable, rational, efficient and economic use of space resources;**
g. **Promote the use of sustainable technology;**
h. **Provide legal certainty and predictability for operators;**
i. **Take into particular account the needs of developing countries;**
j. **Take into particular account the needs of science;**
k. **Take into particular account the contributions of pioneer operators.**

4.3 The international framework should provide that:

a. **Space resources shall be used exclusively for peaceful purposes;**
b. **Space resource activities shall be carried out for the benefit and in the interests of all countries and humankind irrespective of their degree of economic and scientific development;**
c. **Appropriate international consultations shall be undertaken in accordance with Article IX OST(i) if there is a reason to believe that any potentially harmful interference may be caused;**
d. **International cooperation in space resource activities shall be conducted in accordance with international law.**

(i) 1967 Treaty on Principles Governing the Activities of States in the Exploration and Use of Outer Space, including the Moon and Other Celestial Bodies.

2 Explanation

In Building Block 4, the Working Group presented a set of principles for the international framework in three interconnected paragraphs.

The first indicates that consistency with international law ought to be contemplated. Thus, the applicable provisions of international law *de lege lata* should be observed by the framework, in order to assure legal efficiency and consistency. Paragraph 4.1 adopts the general term 'international law' without identifying specific instruments, taking into consideration that some of them are, in fact, not binding by nature. Paragraph 4.1 thus encompasses relevant international space law provisions, requiring compliance with applicable United Nations treaties on outer space as well as other international norms.

Paragraph 4.2 identifies specific principles which should be taken into account when designing the international framework. In total 11 items are mentioned, in letters (a) to (k).

The first, subparagraph (a), supports adherence to the principle of adaptive governance, which envisions that space resource activities should be incrementally regulated, at the appropriate time. During the drafting of all Building Blocks, the principle of adaptive governance was deemed instrumental in allowing for the international framework to retain its relevance throughout the natural evolution of space resource activities.

Subparagraph (b) indicates that both compatibility and predictability of domestic frameworks of States and internal frameworks of international organizations should be promoted, so as to have a more compatible framework at an international level. The wording 'internal' is used because international organizations are entitled to develop their respective regulatory systems. The harmonious co-existence of different domestic and internal frameworks, among each other and in relation to the international framework, is therefore supported. Homogeneity is not, by itself, precluded.

While recognizing the sovereign prerogative of States to legislate in accordance with their national interests, a fundamental tenet of international law, as well as the self-regulatory autonomy of international organizations, subparagraph (b) promotes initiatives toward avoidance of unnecessary conflicts of law. Furthermore, subparagraph (h) takes into consideration the perspectives of operators, highlighting the importance of legal certainty and predictability. This principle is considered of the utmost importance for the industry, given that legal uncertainty as to requirements for mining licenses will influence not only their business models, but also research and development plans.

Contribution to sustainable development is mentioned by subparagraph (c), generally understood, consistent with the definition proposed by the Brundtland Report of 1987, as the development that meets the needs of the present without compromising the ability of future generations to meet their own needs.[9] However, the Working Group considered that there was no need for the Building Blocks to enter in such a level of detail, since applicable principles should be addressed by the appropriate forum when designing the

9 Available at: https://sustainabledevelopment.un.org/content/documents/5987our-common-future.pdf, accessed and verified on 20 December 2019.

international framework. Additionally, the use of sustainable technology is considered by subparagraph (g).

Prevention of disputes arising out of space resource activities is covered in subparagraph (d) from a political and economic standing point. Settlement of disputes is further addressed in Building Block 19.

Working in close connection, subparagraphs (e) and (f) support the orderly and safe utilization of space resources, which should be promoted and secured by the international framework, as well as sustainable, rational, efficient and economic use. The wording adopted was inspired by the International Telecommunication Union (ITU) Constitution and Radio Regulations.

Specific attention should be given to the needs of developing countries, science and pioneer operators, in accordance with subparagraphs (i), (j) and (k). Developing countries, although perhaps not participating in the earlier efforts regarding space resource activities, should have their interests and needs taken into special account, as indicated in subparagraph (i). Building Block 13 reiterates this concern when addressing benefit-sharing mechanisms. Subparagraph (k) recognizes that the interests of pioneer operators, assuming the early risks and burden of a novel and complex space activity, must also be properly acknowledged. Finally, in accordance with subparagraph (j), scientific concerns must not be taken for granted, considering the overarching benefits of enhanced systematic knowledge not only in relation to space resource activities as such, but humankind as a whole. Therefore, certain locations in the solar system should be preserved for the interests of science.

Paragraph 4.3 considers principles which should be contemplated by the international framework, echoing international provisions in force.

Subparagraph (a) states that space resources shall be used exclusively for peaceful purposes, therefore positioning itself in accordance with fundamental tenets of the UN space treaties. This principle has been contemplated by the Building Block in order to safeguard consistency with main provisions of the OST, adopting the same language to maintain coherent phrasing amongst the various legal texts.

Also reflecting the OST, multi-stakeholder perspectives are supported by subparagraph (b), which establishes that space resource activities are to be carried out for the benefit and in the interests of all countries and humankind, regardless of the degree of economic and scientific development of any specific State. Appropriately, this paragraph does not prevent commercial activities in outer space, therefore reiterating its adherence to applicable international principles.

Subparagraph (c) clarifies that whenever potentially harmful interference is believed to be caused, appropriate international consultations should be held, recalling the stipulations of Article IX OST. Thus, a relation is established with Building Block 9, concerning due regard for corresponding interests of all countries and humankind.

Finally, subparagraph (d) supports the principle according to which 'international cooperation in space resource activities shall be conducted in accordance with international law.' During the public commentary period on the draft Building Blocks, the Working Group was asked to provide further clarity and discussion on the role of international cooperation in the development of a future international framework regarding space resource activities, as recognized by this subparagraph.

It is not the role of the Working Group to suggest partnership models for States, as far as space resource activities are concerned; however, it is in the interests of the community to better understand and characterize alternatives through which cooperation might be carried out, so that commonality and transparency in approach, intent, and objectives might be developed. Accordingly, the Socio-Economic Panel focused part of its work on developing and proposing an approach for 'Characterizing International Cooperation Models Related to Space Resources' (see Annex III).

This approach aims to provide a standardized method for describing the actors, forms, objectives and topics involved in space resources related international collaboration. It draws upon work already conducted in multilateral forums, and can be used to describe technical, policy, regulatory and other types of agreement. This common characterization method is intended to support consistency in discussion and exchange of information regarding space resources cooperation, and thus enabling the implementation of Building Block 4.

3 Legal Basis

Different instruments served as the legal basis for Building Block 4, more specifically the OST which, in Article 1, paragraph 1 establishes:

> The exploration and use of outer space, including the Moon and other celestial bodies, shall be carried out for the benefit and in the interests of all countries, irrespective of their degree of economic or scientific development, and shall be the province of all mankind.

That is also the principle of paragraph 1 of the Declaration of Legal Principles:

> The exploration and use of outer space shall be carried on for the benefit and in the interests of all mankind.

For the States Parties to the MA, its Article 4 contains a similar provision in paragraph 1:

> The exploration and use of the Moon shall be the province of all mankind and shall be carried out for the benefit and in the interests of all countries, irrespective of their degree of economic or scientific development. Due regard shall be paid to the interests of present and future generations as well as to the need to promote higher standards of living and conditions of economic and social progress and development in accordance with the Charter of the United Nations.

Also related to Building Block 4, Article III OST characterizes the applicability of international law to space activities in general:

> States Parties to the Treaty shall carry on activities in the exploration and use of outer space, including the Moon and other celestial bodies, in accordance with international law, including the Charter of the United Nations, in the interest of maintaining international peace and security and promoting international cooperation and understanding.

Article III OST codified the rule introduced by paragraph 1.a, of the United Nations General Assembly Resolution 1721 A (XVI), of 1961, and later by paragraph 4 Declaration of Legal Principles, as follows:

> The activities of States in the exploration and use of outer space shall be carried on in accordance with international law, including the Charter of the United Nations, in the interest of maintaining international peace and security and promoting international cooperation and understanding.

International cooperation in the exploration and use of outer space was addressed by United Nations General Assembly Resolution 51/122, 1966, which declared, in its first paragraph:

> International cooperation in the exploration and use of outer space for peaceful purposes (hereafter 'international cooperation') shall be conducted in accordance with the provisions of international law, including the Charter of the United Nations and the Treaty on the Principles Governing the Activities of States in the Exploration and Use of Outer Space, including the Moon and Other Celestial Bodies. It shall be carried out for the benefit and in the interest of all States, irrespective of their degree of economic, social or scientific and technological development, and shall be the province of all mankind. Particular account should be taken of the needs of developing countries.

Regarding the conduct of space activities in accordance with international law, for the States Parties to the MA, Article 2 provides that:

> All activities on the Moon, including its exploration and use, shall be carried out in accordance with international law, in particular the Charter of the United Nations, and taking into account the Declaration on Principles of International Law concerning Friendly Relations and Cooperation among States in accordance with the Charter of the United Nations, adopted by the General Assembly on 24 October 1970, in the interest of maintaining peace and security and promoting international cooperation and mutual understanding, and with due regard to the corresponding interests of all other States Parties.

The principle of cooperation and mutual assistance, with due regard to corresponding interests, is covered by Article XI OST:

> In the exploration and use of outer space, including the Moon and other celestial bodies, States Parties to the Treaty shall be guided by the principle of cooperation and mutual assistance and shall conduct all their activities in outer space, including the Moon and other celestial bodies, with due regard to the corresponding interests of all other States Parties to the Treaty. States Parties to the Treaty shall pursue studies of outer space, including the Moon and other celestial bodies, and conduct exploration of them so as to avoid their harmful contamination and also adverse changes in the environment of the Earth resulting from the introduction of extraterrestrial matter and, where necessary, shall adopt appropriate measures for this purpose. If a State Party to the Treaty has reason to believe that an activity or experiment planned by it or its nationals in outer space, including the Moon and other celestial bodies, would cause potentially harmful interference with activities of other States Parties in the peaceful exploration and use of outer space, including the Moon and other celestial bodies, it shall undertake appropriate international consultations before proceeding with any such activity or experiment. A State Party to the Treaty which has reason to believe that an activity or experiment planned by another State Party in outer space, including the Moon and other celestial bodies, would cause potentially harmful interference with activities in the peaceful exploration and use of outer space, including the Moon and other celestial bodies, may request consultation concerning the activity or experiment.

This rule has its origins in another principle of the Declaration of Legal Principles, included in its paragraph 6:

> In the exploration and use of outer space, States shall be guided by the principle of cooperation and mutual assistance and shall conduct all their activities in outer space with due regard for the corresponding interests of other States. If a State has reason to believe that an outer space activity or experiment planned by it or its nationals would cause potentially harmful interference with activities of other States in the peaceful exploration and use of outer space, it shall undertake appropriate international consultations before proceeding with any such activity or experiment. A State which has reason to believe that an outer space activity or experiment planned by another State would cause potentially harmful interference with activities in the peaceful exploration and use of outer space may request consultation concerning the activity or experiment.

For the States Parties to the MA, this principle is reflected in its Article 4, paragraph 2, addressing cooperation and mutual assistance:

> States Parties shall be guided by the principle of cooperation and mutual assistance in all their activities concerning the exploration and use of the Moon. International cooperation in pursuance of this Agreement should be as wide as possible and may take place on a multilateral basis, on a bilateral basis or through international intergovernmental organizations.

Regarding interference, Article 8, paragraph 3 MA reads that:

> Activities of States Parties in accordance with paragraphs 1 and 2 of this article shall not interfere with the activities of other States Parties on the Moon. When such interference may occur, the States Parties concerned shall undertake consultations in accordance with article 15, paragraphs 2 and 3, of this Agreement

Moreover, Article 5, paragraph 2 MA provides that:

> If a State becomes aware that another State Party plans to operate simultaneously in the same area of or in the same orbit around or trajectory to or around the Moon, it shall promptly inform the other State of the timing of and plans for its own operations.

Due to its similar spirit, reference should be made to the ITU Constitution, Article 44, paragraph 2, which states:

> In using frequency bands for radio services, Member States shall bear in mind that radio frequencies and any associated orbits, including the geostationary-satellite orbit, are limited natural resources and that they must be used rationally, efficiently and economically, in conformity with the provisions of the Radio Regulations, so that countries or groups of countries may have equitable access to those orbits and frequencies, taking into account the special needs of the developing countries and the geographical situation of particular countries.

The provision on the exclusively peaceful character of space resource activities was inspired by Article IV OST, which states that 'the Moon and other celestial bodies' shall be used exclusively for peaceful purposes. Adopting a comparative approach, relevant provisions may be identified in other international instruments regulating the exploration and use of international territories, beyond national sovereignty. The Antarctica Treaty, in its Article 1, paragraph 1, states that 'Antarctica shall be used for peaceful purposes only.' In similar terms, the United Nations Convention on the Law of the Seas provides, in its Article 88, that 'the high seas shall be reserved for peaceful purposes.'

4 *Alternatives Discussed*

Building Block 4 was drafted during the first face-to-face meeting, in April 2016. The provision was originally significantly smaller, containing less principles. The members and observers did not consider this Building Block particularly contentious, and rather focused on improving its wording.

Regarding paragraph 4.1, the only issue raised was whether or not it should specify which laws, in particular, the international framework should be consistent with, some taking the position that instruments such as the UN Charter or the UN treaties on outer space should be mentioned.

Regarding paragraph 4.2, a proposal was made to introduce an autonomous principle concerning the appropriate timing for the commencement of the international framework itself, as well as a suggestion to assure that international recognized rights of all humans apply to humans living and working in space, were made, but not accepted. Additionally, a proposal was made to specifically mention public and private interests, as to be taken into account.

Concerning the subparagraphs of this provision, discussions were held in relation to subparagraph (a) as to whether the international framework would be necessary before the activity effectively takes place, as well as an earlier position that the adaptive governance principle was also applicable to potential future space resource activities.

Regarding subparagraph (b), the main alternatives concerned the use of the wording 'compatibility' or alternatives, such as 'consistent' or 'development'. In relation to subparagraphs (c) and (f), although concerning different principles, both had their discussion revolve more around the definition of 'sustainable' and, in the latter case, also 'rational', 'efficient' and 'economic', with member and observers offering different inputs as to their meaning and other legal instruments which could contribute to proper definition.

On subparagraph (e), the only alternative discussed was the proposed deletion of the term 'orderly', as it could indicate a first-come-first-served basis. Discussions related to subparagraph (h) addressed whether in addition to operators, owners and shareholders of private companies should also be included.

In respect of subparagraph (i), some members and observers were of the opinion that the term 'developing countries' could be considered as anachronist, and suggestions were made to replace it with other terms such as 'emerging space powers' or 'all countries', but these were eventually not adopted by the Working Group.

As for paragraph 4.3, besides a brief suggestion to explicitly mention commercial utilization in subparagraph (a), the most discussed provisions were the ones related to harmful interference, included in subparagraphs (c) and (d). Some members were of the opinion that the threshold of 'harmful' should not be set by the Building Block, considering that such a limitation would raise debates as to when an interference would in fact be deemed as such. Additionally, a view was expressed that Article IV of the Outer Space Treaty does not expressly stipulate that space resources shall be used exclusively for peaceful purposes, questioning the interpretation of said provision.

Finally, during the last meeting in November 2019, subparagraph (d) of paragraph 4.3, which stated that 'space resource activities shall not harmfully interfere with other on-going space activities, including other space resource activities', was excluded, due to lack of understanding of the applicable *lex lata.* On the one hand, it was expressed that Article IX OST does not create an obligation of result, in that States have to ensure that their activities will not cause harmful interference, but an obligation of conduct. In particular, the understanding behind the initial formulation of Building Block 4.3 subparagraph (c) was that States should not knowingly allow their authorized activities to cause harmful interference, a concept expressly established in the Corfu Channel case, which was mentioned as prominent example. On the other hand, it was supported that the previous formulation, reading 'space resource activities shall not harmfully interfere with other on-going space activities', would go beyond the scope of Article IX OST that only provides for consultations in case of eminent harmful interference. In any event, the monitoring and redressing of harmful impact, as well as the due regard to corresponding interests of all countries form the subject of Building Block 12 and 9 respectively, where the formulation of the text reflected the aforementioned division in an appropriate manner. Following the removal of subparagraphs (c), the remaining subparagraphs were renumbered.

5 International Responsibility for Space Resource Activities

1 *Text*

The international framework should provide that:

a. **States shall bear international responsibility for national space resource activities, whether such activities are carried out by governmental agencies or non-governmental entities, and for ensuring that such activities are carried out in conformity with the international framework;**
b. **Non-governmental space resource activities shall require prior authorization and continuing supervision by the appropriate State;**
c. **When space resource activities are carried out by an international organization, responsibility for compliance with the international framework shall be borne by the international organization and by the States participating in such organization.**

2 *Explanation*

International responsibility applicable to space resource activities is contemplated by Building Block 5, which reflects not only general international law but also particular features of space law instruments, more specifically Article VI OST.

The Building Block suggests that the international framework should provide for three different, although interrelated, aspects of international responsibility, presented in subparagraphs (a) to (c).

The first, in subparagraph (a), is the attributability of national space resource activities to States, irrespective of whether they are governmental or non-governmental in nature. This responsibility also entails that States ensure that national space activities are carried out in conformity with the international framework.

The second aspect covered by Building Block 5, closely linked to the previous one, is the requirement of authorization and supervision by the appropriate State of non-governmental space resource activities. States are internationally responsible for non-governmental space resource activities, and subparagraph (b) confirms that appropriate procedures must be put in place.

Finally, in relation to space resource activities performed by international organizations, subparagraph (c) provides that international responsibility for compliance with the framework in questions shall be borne not only by the international organizations themselves, as separate, autonomous subjects of international law, but also by their Member States. Therefore, States should be aware that international organizations may not be used as a means to circumvent their responsibility as members, as far as space resource activities are concerned.

3 *Legal Basis*

Any legal system confers not only rights to their subjects, but also duties. Thus, international responsibility of States constitutes a fundamental principle of general international law, based on their sovereign equality. Indeed, all international legal subjects, including States and international organizations, can be held responsible for their behavior, as supported by international jurisprudence.

The specific structure of Building Block 5 was designed to add clarity to its provisions, but both in language and content it closely follows Article VI OST, which formulates international responsibility of States for national activities in outer space as follows:

> States Parties to the Treaty shall bear international responsibility for national activities in outer space, including the Moon and other celestial bodies, whether such activities are carried on by governmental agencies or by non-governmental entities, and for assuring that national activities are carried out in conformity with the provisions set forth in the present Treaty. The activities of non-governmental entities in outer space, including the Moon and other celestial bodies, shall require authorization and continuing supervision by the appropriate State Party to the Treaty. When activities are carried on in outer space, including the Moon and other celestial bodies, by an international organization, responsibility for compliance with this Treaty shall be borne both by the international organization and by the States Parties to the Treaty participating in such organization.

For the States Parties to the MA, international responsibility is addressed in Article 14, paragraph 1.

> States Parties to this Agreement shall bear international responsibility for national activities on the Moon, whether such activities are carried on by governmental agencies or by non-governmental entities, and for assuring that national activities are carried out in conformity with the provisions set forth in this Agreement. States Parties shall ensure that non-governmental entities under their jurisdiction shall engage in activities on the Moon only under the authority and continuing supervision of the appropriate State.

Article 16 MA extends the application of the provisions referring to States to international intergovernmental organizations.

Article VI OST and Article 14 MA were based on paragraph 5 Declaration of Legal Principles:

> States bear international responsibility for national activities in outer space, whether carried on by governmental agencies or by non-governmental entities, and for assuring that national activities are carried on in conformity with the principles set forth in the present Declaration. The activities of non-governmental entities in outer space shall require authorization and continuing supervision by the State concerned. When activities are carried on in outer space by an international organization, responsibility for compliance with the principles set forth in this Declaration shall be borne by the international organization and by the States participating in it.

Many States have implemented national legislation detailing the process for authorizing and supervising outer space activities. Specific reference may be made to the laws of the USA[10] and Luxembourg,[11] as far as space resource activities are concerned.

4 *Alternatives Discussed*

Building Block 5 was drafted to reflect the legal principles contained in Article VI OST. In general, the content remained uncontentious during the Working Group meetings, with most of the discussion revolving around the choice of words. Over time, the discussions, progressed from matters involving jurisdiction toward those related to responsibility, as applicable to space resource activities.

It was suggested that specific mechanisms for implementing the topic of this Building Block constituted a matter for national law and should be acknowledged as such. Also, it was argued that the UN treaties on outer space already covered the international responsibility in relation to space activities in general, which would inevitably encompass space resource activities. Nevertheless, the Working Group decided in favor of establishing a specific provision on that regard, following, as close as possible, applicable international instruments in effect. During the April 2019 meeting, it was decided to develop an autonomous entry for jurisdiction and control over space-made products used in space resource activities, which became Building Block 6.

10 US Commercial Space Launch Competitiveness Act, 2015.

11 Loi sur l'Exploration et l'Utilisation des Ressources de l'Espace, 2017.

6 JURISDICTION AND CONTROL OVER SPACE-MADE PRODUCTS USED IN SPACE RESOURCE ACTIVITIES

1 Text

The international framework should provide that States have jurisdiction and control over any space-made products used in the space resource activities for which they are responsible.

2 Explanation

State jurisdiction and control over space-made products used in space resource activities are covered in Building Block 6, which mirrors Article VIII OST. Accordingly, as a direct consequence of the international responsibility of States addressed in Building Block 5, Building Block 6 states that the international framework should provide for proper authority and supervision to be specifically exercised over space-based products.

In international law, jurisdiction is understood as the power or legal competence of practicing State functions. Reflecting the concept of sovereignty, jurisdiction is a prerogative reserved solely for States, and is based on the principle of effectiveness. Extraterritorial jurisdiction, *i.e.* jurisdiction over persons, property or events beyond national borders, requires close connection between the State and its subject, and may lead to international conflicts. Since jurisdiction is not based on exclusiveness, occasionally acts may be under the realm of more than one State. On the other hand, cases involving negative conflicts of jurisdiction, where no State consider itself competent, may lead to challenging situations involving denial of justice or responsibility. Overlapping or concurring claims are usually regulated by private international law, which addresses both positive and negative conflicts of jurisdiction.

On the other hand, the notion of control implies actual and continuous authoritative influence over something or someone, as well as the ability to manage or direct it. Such operational capacity may be exercised even remotely, by relying on the power of obedience or specific technical capabilities.

A mechanism for jurisdiction, control and corresponding responsibility is necessary for the maintenance of law and order in outer space. Therefore, a chain of attribution related to space-made products is to be established, identifying the respective State whose laws are applicable in any given scenario. 'Space-made product', as defined by Building Block 2, paragraph 5, is considered a 'product made in outer space wholly or partially from space resources.' As clarified in the commentary to that provision, the Working Group considers that this excludes raw mineral and volatile materials, including water, irrespective of form.

There is a close connection between Building Block 6 and the preceding one, Building Block 5, dealing with 'international responsibility for space resource activities'. Both were originally considered in conjunction, as attested by their evolution from earlier drafts up to the final document. Building Block 6 provides a mechanism for jurisdiction and control in relation to space-made products, ensuring the identification of the internationally responsible State in accordance with Building Block 5, and therefore enables the liability regime considered by Building Block 15.

3 Legal Basis

In accordance with the non-appropriation of outer space principle of Article II OST,

> outer space, including the Moon and other celestial bodies, is not subject to national appropriation by claim of sovereignty, by means of use or occupation, or by any other means.

Yet, jurisdiction may be exercised by States in outer space, over space objects and personnel. Space-based products, when in outer space and therefore beyond national limits, may be subject to extraterritorial jurisdiction, provided that a relevant link with a State is established.

Article VIII OST states:

> A State Party to the Treaty on whose registry an object launched into outer space is carried shall retain jurisdiction and control over such object, and over any personnel thereof, while in outer space or on a celestial body. Ownership of objects launched into outer space, including objects landed or constructed on a celestial body, and of their component parts, is not affected by their presence in outer space or on a celestial body or by their return to the Earth. Such objects or component parts found beyond the limits of the State Party to the Treaty on whose registry they are carried shall be returned to that State Party, which shall, upon request, furnish identifying data prior to their return.

Article VIII OST refers to both private and State ownership, since no distinction is made on that regard. The property law applicable to the space object in question is usually that of the State of registry, which enjoys corresponding jurisdiction and control. Nevertheless, attention should be granted to the applicable municipal law, in order to identify specific provisions.

This article was based on paragraph 7 Declaration of Legal Principles:

> The State on whose registry an object launched into outer space is carried shall retain jurisdiction and control over such object, and any personnel thereon, while in outer space. Ownership of objects launched into outer space, and of their component parts, is not affected by their passage through outer space or by their return to the Earth. Such objects or component parts found beyond the limits of the State of registry shall be returned to that State, which shall furnish identifying data upon request prior to return.

As far as the Moon and other celestial bodies are concerned, Article 12 MA clarifies that jurisdiction and control is kept in relation to personnel, vehicles, equipment, facilities, stations and installations. In accordance with its text:

> States Parties shall retain jurisdiction and control over their personnel, vehicles, equipment, facilities, stations and installations on the Moon. The ownership of space vehicles, equipment, facilities, stations and installations shall not be affected by their presence on the Moon.

4 *Alternatives Discussed*

Building Blocks 5 and 6 were initially considered by the Working Group as a single and unified structure. However, during the April 2019 meeting, it was decided to split them in two autonomous Building Blocks, in order to distinguish between responsibility and jurisdiction applicable to space resource activities. The decision further mirrors the OST, which similarly divides these issues between Articles VI and Article VIII.

During the debates, a view was expressed that jurisdiction and control is more closely connected to rights than obligations, based on interpretation of Article VIII OST. Accordingly, it was indicated that whenever two or more States are responsible for a certain space resources activity, for instance, in an international cooperative project, in general only one of them should have jurisdiction and control over the respective space-made product.

Discussions also emerged over word choice and relevant concepts, in particular 'responsible' vs 'appropriate' with regard to the State exercising jurisdiction and control. Concerns were raised over applying general rules applicable to space objects to a 'space-made product', which led to a specific reference to the latter. Finally, the link between an operator and its respective State, ultimately a matter for national law, was considered as benefiting from regulatory consistency at the international level.

In the framework of jurisdiction and control, the point of responsibility for space-made products was raised. Given that OST does not provide specifically for such responsibility, hence the issue was not addressed in the Building Blocks, it is not the intention of the Working Group that this legal gap would allow States to escape such responsibility.

After discussions on the concurrent jurisdiction and related matters, the final wording of Building Block 6 was accorded, with minor modifications, during the meeting of November 2019.

7 Priority Rights

1 *Text*

The international framework should enable the attribution of priority rights to an operator to search for and/or recover space resources for a maximum period of time and a maximum area upon registration in an international registry, and provide for the international recognition of such priority rights. The attribution, duration, and the area of the priority right should be determined on the basis of the specific circumstances of a proposed space resource activity.

2 *Explanation*

Priority rights are introduced in Building Block 7 as a fundamental mechanism to ensure proper development of space resource activities, in accordance with international law. Time-limited and triggered by proper registration in an international registry, priority rights are to be granted to operators in relation to search of space resources and/or their recovery.

Since international law prevents States from appropriating outer space, including celestial bodies, by claim of sovereignty, use, occupation or any other means, space resource activities should rely on the granting of priority rights, attributed by registration in an international registry according to applicable procedure and criteria.

The attribution of priority rights is considered necessary to protect the effort and investment of the operator in locating space resources and developing corresponding activities, as well as to coordinate access to resources, so as to avoid harmful interference with the activities of other operators.

Building Block 7 indicates that the international framework should not only contemplate and regulate those rights, but also provide for their international recognition. The establishment and maintenance of publicly available international registry, addressed in Building Block 18, is thus essential for the attribution of priority rights for space resource activities.

Considering not only the attribution of priority rights, but also the applicable duration and area of effect, their determination should be based on the particular, actual circumstances involving the space resource activity in question. Therefore, standard or universal procedures are not covered by this Building Block, and should, in due time, be considered by the international framework.

3 Legal Basis

Access to space resources, as in relation to outer space in general, including the Moon and other celestial bodies, is freely granted by the OST in accordance with Article 1, paragraph 2:

> Outer space, including the Moon and other celestial bodies, shall be free for exploration and use by all States without discrimination of any kind, on a basis of equality and in accordance with international law, and there shall be free access to all areas of celestial bodies.

Likewise, for the States Parties to the MA, Article 11, paragraph 2 provides that:

> States Parties have the right to exploration and use of the Moon without discrimination of any kind, on the basis of equality and in accordance with international law and the terms of this Agreement

Regarding the freedom of exploration and use, the MA further specifies in Article 8, paragraph 1, that:

> States Parties may pursue their activities in the exploration and use of the Moon anywhere on or below its surface, subject to the provisions of this Agreement.

The principle of freedom of access was included in the United Nations General Assembly Resolution 1721 A (XVI), of 1961, paragraph 1 (b), which states:

> Outer space and celestial bodies are free for exploration and use by all States in conformity with international law and are not subject to national appropriation.

Another international instrument, the Declaration of Legal Principles, as its paragraph 2, incorporated this position in accordance with the following text:

> Outer space and celestial bodies are free for exploration and use by all States on a basis of equality and in accordance with international law.

Furthermore, adopting a comparative approach, since radio frequencies and any associated orbits, including the geostationary satellite orbit, are considered as limited natural resource by Article 44 of the Constitution of the International Telecommunication Union (ITU),[12] a priority rights system was internationally established in relation to certain orbital positions and the corresponding frequencies, in accordance with the ITU Radio Regulations. In order to prevent harmful interference between radio stations of different countries, the allocation of bands of radio-frequency spectrum and the procedures for avoiding this interference are also regulated by the ITU.

4 *Alternatives Discussed*

Two analogous regimes were particularly considered by the Working Group in relation to the attribution of priority rights for space resource activities: the ITU system applicable to the geostationary orbit and the UNCLOS system for deep seabed resources. Ultimately, Building Block 7 tended towards the ITU system, partially because of it being part of the corpus of space law, but also due to concerns over difficulties related to UNCLOS.

Furthermore, there was discussion about the exclusivity and duration of priority rights; a position was presented advocating the need to consider the requirements of space law (*i.e.* Articles I and II OST) as well as the needs of industry, enabling private actors to be reasonably secure in their ability to pursue a return on their investment.

During earlier versions, Building Block 7 included reference according to which the international framework should provide that priority rights were to be attributed to an

---

12 *In using frequency bands for radio services, Member States shall bear in mind that radio frequencies and any associated orbits, including the geostationary-satellite orbit, are limited natural resources and that they must be used rationally, efficiently and economically, in conformity with the provisions of the Radio Regulations, so that countries or groups of countries may have equitable access to those orbits and frequencies, taking account the special needs of the developing countries and the geographical situation of particular countries.* Constitution of the International Telecommunication Union, 22 December 1992, 1825 UNTS 330.

operator to search and/or recover space resources *in situ* for a maximum period of time and a maximum area upon registration in an international registry. Further discussing this provision, it was acknowledged that the mere use of remote sensing capabilities for identification of space resources in celestial bodies would not suffice for the attribution of priority rights to an operator. In this regard, the Working Group recognized that the purpose of priority rights in the context of Building Block 7 aims to protect the operators which perform physical, rather than remote, research, given that they would contribute technological and financial capital to perform *in situ* research. Therefore, priority rights to search for resources would enable these operators to safeguard their research missions. At the same time, the Working Group noted that remote sensing should not fall under the scope of the Building Blocks, since it is regulated by other instruments, which do not provide for priority in remote sensing and are mainly designed to prevent signal interference among remote sensing activities. Major changes to the structure of Building Block 7 were agreed during the session of April 2019, leading to the formulation finally agreed.

As reflected in the final sentence of Building Block 7, discussions were held about the need for specific processes for particular celestial bodies, recognizing the differences between the Moon and asteroids.

There were considerable debates on the needs of developing states and the inadequacy of the principle of 'first come first served' to ensure their protection, as well as pioneering interests and perspectives on that regard. It was argued that this principle constituted the most effective method for the initial stage of the space resources industry. Finally, it was accepted that the UNCLOS process of reserving areas exclusively for developing states should not be incorporated in the Building Blocks.

A view was expressed that priority rights, irrespective of its connection to space resources, could eventually be transferred to third parties, in accordance with provisions to be progressively determined by national law or international agreements.

Talks took place on whether authorizing States should be required to ensure the feasibility of the proposed activities; however, the Working Group decided to leave this for later discussion by the proper authorities, in due time.

Finally, during the meeting of November 2019, the title of Building Block 7, originally 'Access to Space Resources', was replaced by 'Priority Rights', in order to better reflect its content and subject matter.

8 Resource Rights

1 Text

8.1 The international framework should ensure that resource rights over raw mineral and volatile materials extracted from space resources, as well as products derived therefrom, can lawfully be acquired through domestic legislation, bilateral agreements and/or multilateral agreements.
8.2 The international framework should enable the mutual recognition between States of such resource rights.
8.3 The international framework should ensure that the utilization of space resources is carried out in accordance with the principle of non-appropriation under Article II OST.

2 Explanation

Resource rights are the subject of Building Block 8, devoted to the utilization of space resources. Applicable to raw mineral and volatile materials extracted from space resources, along with any possible derivative product, those rights should be ensured by the envisioned international framework, allowing them to be lawfully acquired. This provision is meant to address the commercialization of space resources, which necessarily relies on the acquisition of legal rights over the materials extracted and the products derived therefrom.

Such rights may be granted by virtue of domestic legislation, bilateral or multilateral agreements, as acknowledged by paragraph 8.2. Additionally, paragraph 8.2 stipulates that mutual recognition between States of resource rights should be contemplated and confirmed by the international framework, thus creating an enabling environment for space resource activities.

In order to ensure the lawful utilization of space resources, paragraph 8.3 reiterates the importance of consistency with international law, already covered in paragraph 4.1 of Building Block 4. Attention is drawn to Article II OST, which formulates the principle of non-appropriation, according to which outer space, including the Moon and other celestial bodies, is indelibly declared not be subjected to national appropriation. Paragraph 8.2 states that this fundamental rule should be acknowledged and promoted by the international framework, ensuring that the utilization of space resources is conducted in accordance with international law. In order to ensure compliance with international space law, the Working Group also took into account the provisions of the MA, thus carefully formulating the language of Building Block 8 so as not to conflict with the text of that agreement.

There is a clear relationship between matters applicable to the utilization of space resources as provided in Building Block 8, and those involving access to space resources, including priority rights, as addressed in Building Block 7.

3 *Legal Basis*

The main legal basis for Building Block 8 is Article I, paragraph 2 OST, which provides:

> Outer space, including the Moon and other celestial bodies, shall be free for exploration and use by all States, without discrimination of any kind, on a basis of equality and in accordance with international law.

The referred provisions followed paragraph 2 of the Declaration of Legal Principles, according to which:

> Outer space and celestial bodies are free for exploration and use by all States on a basis of equality and in accordance with international law.

Building Block 8 implements the freedom to 'use' outer space through the acquisition of resource rights over raw mineral and volatile material extracted from space resources. It also fosters the utilization of outer space 'without discrimination of any kind, on a basis of equality and in accordance with international law', through the provision of mutual recognition among resource rights, which removes any political discretion and grants the same treatment to everyone, subject only to reciprocity, thus achieving the non-discrimination principle mandated by the OST.

On this point, Building Block 8 is also meant to implement Article IX OST, which *inter alia* provides that

> In the exploration and use of outer space, including the Moon and other celestial bodies, States Parties to the Treaty shall by guided by the principle of co-operation and mutual assistance.

Accordingly, because it is based on reciprocal trust, mutual recognition has successfully been applied to enhance international cooperation in the area of trade, with specific reference to the free movement of goods.

Reference is expressly identified in relation to Article II OST, which codified the principle of non-appropriation in the following terms:

> Outer space, including the Moon and other celestial bodies, is not subject to national appropriation by claim of sovereignty, by means of use or occupation, or by any other means.

The OST followed the non-appropriation principle as acknowledged by both the United Nations General Assembly Resolutions Resolution 1721 A (XVI), of 1961, and 1962 (XVIII), 1963. The latter stated, in paragraph 3:

> Outer space and celestial bodies are not subject to national appropriation by claim of sovereignty, by means of use or occupation, or by any other means.

The principle of non-appropriation of outer space is one of the most cardinal tenets of international space law, and must be duly acknowledged in order to ensure proper access to space resources. Based not only in treaty but also in international customary law, the principle prohibits the national appropriation of territories in outer space, including celestial bodies.

Likewise, for the States Parties to the MA, the non-appropriation principle is incorporated in its Article 11, paragraph 2:

> The Moon is not subject to national appropriation by any claim of sovereignty, by means of use or occupation, or by any other means.[13]

Furthermore, paragraph 3 of Article 11 of the MA establishes that:

> Neither the surface not the subsurface of the Moon, not any part thereof or natural resources in place, shall become property of any State, international intergovernmental organization or non-governmental organization, national organization or non-governmental entity or of any natural person. The placement of personnel, space vehicles, equipment, facilities, stations and installations on or below the surface of the Moon, including structures connected with its surface or subsurface, shall not create a right of ownership over the surface or the subsurface of the Moon or any areas thereof.

In the scope of Building Block 8, particular attention should be drawn to the last sentence of paragraph 3 of Article 11 MA, according to which:

---

13 In accordance with Article 1, paragraph 2, for the purposes of the MA *reference to the Moon shall include orbits around or other trajectories to or around it.*

> The foregoing provisions are without prejudice to the international regime referred in paragraph 5 of this article.

Paragraph 5 of Article 11 MA provides that:

> States Parties to this Agreement hereby undertake to establish an international regime, including appropriate procedures, to govern the exploitation of the natural resources of the Moon as such exploitation is about to become feasible. This provision shall be implemented in accordance with article 18 of this Agreement.

4 Alternatives Discussed

The Building Block regarding utilization of space resources was introduced for open discussion at the Working Group during its first face-to-face meeting in April 2016. Since then, it has been partially rephrased to reflect the outcome of debates among members and observers, as well as suggestions received from the general public. Ultimately, the Working Group reached consensus over the final structure of this Building Block at the face-to-face meeting of April 2019.

Inter alia, Building Block 8 has experienced successive changes, reflecting considerable debates within the Working Group. In the first paragraph, the term 'internationally recognized property rights' has been changed with the current terminology, which refers to 'resource rights' and 'mutual recognition between States'. In the last paragraph, the statement advocating for the legality of the full utilization of a celestial body has been abandoned in favor of a direct reference to the non-appropriation principle of Article II OST.

The rationale behind these decisions can be summarized as follows. First, the term 'resource rights' was chosen instead of 'property rights', since it was agreed that it was not for the Working Group to decide what legal content shall be assigned to the rights eventually granted over space resources. Likewise, the provision of 'international' recognition seemed too dogmatic when compared to the effect of 'mutual' recognition, which allows States to recognize foreign resource rights on a basis of reciprocity, rather than because of an absolute obligation to do so. Lastly, based on the principle of adaptive governance, the Working Group concluded that it was not necessary to assess the legality of the complex future utilization of celestial bodies at this point in time. On the contrary, a direct reference to one of the cornerstones of international space law, being interpreted as it may, seemed a more appropriate solution.

Further to that, it was debated whether or not Building Block 8 should make reference to the UNCLOS regime governing the utilization of the deep seabed. Ultimately, the Working Group decided not to mention this regime, since its suitability for the regulation of space resource activities is still contested among States and scholars.

The Working Group considered whether resource rights should be included in an international registry or reciprocally accepted through mutual recognition. In the end, mutual recognition was preferred as a simpler and more effective cooperation tool.

Discussion evolved around the question whether the final paragraph of Building Block 8 should explicitly refer to Article II OST or simply mention the non-appropriation principle. In favor of this proposal, it was pointed out that not all States are parties to the OST and the treaty could eventually be amended or superseded, thus compromising the future relevance of this provision. The Working Group decided to maintain the reference to Article II OST, mostly because of the universal recognition among States and scholars that this provision is declaratory of customary international law.

As far as the last paragraph is concerned, a previous version suggested that the international framework provides for the mutual recognition of resource rights. However, it was pointed out that such recognition would be a matter subject to the legislative sovereignty of a State and should not be dictated by an international framework. Nevertheless, the Working Group acknowledged the significance of mutual recognition of priority rights and proceeded to revise Building Block 8 accordingly.

During the meeting of November 2019, a reference regarding the lawful acquisition of resource rights 'through domestic legislation, bilateral agreements and/or multilateral agreements' was added to Building Block 8.1. Moreover, a new paragraph 8.2 was created, severing the final part of the original paragraph 8.1, to clarify that the mutual recognition of resource rights between States should be enabled by the international framework. As a consequence, the last paragraph was renumbered as 8.3. Finally, the former title of Building Block 8, 'Utilization of Space Resources', was replaced by 'Resource Rights', to better reflect its substance.

9 Due Regard for Corresponding Interests of all Countries and Humankind

1 Text

The international framework should provide that States and international organizations responsible for space resource activities shall give due regard to the corresponding interests of all countries and humankind.

2 *Explanation*

The corresponding interests of all countries, as well as of humankind, *vis-à-vis* space resource activities, are the subject matter of Building Block 9. The international framework is advised to specifically contemplate that States and international organizations, responsible for space resource activities, shall take into consideration multiple perspectives on space resource activities.

Building Block 9 deals with the principle of due regard, which in international law refers to the performance of an act with a certain standard of care, attention or observance. Accordingly, Building Block 9 provides that, under the international framework, States and international organizations responsible for space resource activities shall be subject to the due regard obligation, and determines its benchmark in the corresponding interests of all countries and humankind.

By considering a vast geographical scope, without any limitations, Building Block 9 reinstates the magnitude of the international framework in question, and its implications to the international community. Indeed, the provision acknowledges the wide global impacts expected from space resource activities, requiring appropriate attention from those engaged in them.

Notably, Building Block 9 distinguishes between all countries and humankind to reflect the contemporary architecture of the global society, which is no longer composed solely by sovereign States but also by governmental and non-governmental entities representing the many facets of social interaction. Like in various other Building Blocks the gender-neutral term 'humankind' was adopted in Building Block 9 instead of 'mankind' used in the OST, to further illustrate its inclusiveness.

3 *Legal Basis*

Building Block 9 follows Article I, paragraph 1 OST which provides that the exploration and use of outer space must be carried out for the general benefit and considering wide-ranging interests:

> The exploration and use of outer space, including the Moon and other celestial bodies, shall be carried out for the benefit and in the interests of all countries, irrespective of their degree of economic or scientific development, and shall be the province of all mankind.

The term 'province of mankind' is not defined by this provision, and its meaning remains subject to international debates.

The basis of the referred position can be found, although in more concise wording, in paragraph 1 of the Declaration of Legal Principles, as follows:

> The exploration and use of outer space shall be carried on for the benefit and in the interests of all mankind.

For the States Parties to the MA, its Article 4 adopts similar language, reflecting a wide-ranging scope, in its paragraph 1:

> The exploration and use of the Moon shall be the province of all mankind and shall be carried out for the benefit and in the interests of all countries, irrespective of their degree of economic or scientific development. Due regard shall be paid to the interests of present and future generations as well as to the need to promote higher standards of living and conditions of economic and social progress and development in accordance with the Charter of the United Nations.

As far as other space activities are concerned, Principle II of Resolution 41/65, 1986, regarding 'Principles Related to Remote Sensing of the Earth from Space' is based on similar grounds:

> Remote sensing activities shall be carried out for the benefit and in the interests of all countries, irrespective of their degree of economic, social or scientific and technological development, and taking into particular consideration the needs of the developing countries.

Building Block 9 is also based on Article IX OST, which provides:

> In the exploration and use of outer space, including the Moon and other celestial bodies, States Parties to the Treaty shall be guided by the principle of cooperation and mutual assistance and shall conduct all their activities in outer space, including the Moon and other celestial bodies, with due regard to the corresponding interests of all other States Parties to the Treaty. [...]

The OST followed paragraph 6 Declaration of Legal Principles, which espoused this principle in the following passage:

> In the exploration and use of outer space, States shall be guided by the principle of cooperation and mutual assistance and shall conduct all their activities in outer space with due regard for the corresponding interests of other States.

Finally, paragraph 1 of Article 4 MA ventured in the same direction by stating:

> The exploration and use of the Moon shall be the province of all mankind and shall be carried out for the benefit and in the interests of all countries, irrespective of their degree of economic or scientific development. Due regard shall be paid to the interests of present and future generations as well as to the need to promote higher standards of living and conditions of economic and social progress and development in accordance with the Charter of the United Nations.

In relation to the term 'due regard', reference is made to a recent case from the International Tribunal for the Law of the Sea, where the term appears for the first time in a Court's decision and is defined by one of the parties as the obligation of States, when exercising their freedoms, to consider the interests of other States and refrain from interfering with other States exercising the same freedoms.[14]

4 *Alternatives Discussed*

The Building Block mandating due regard for the corresponding interests of other States was introduced for open discussion at the Working Group during its third face-to-face meeting in April 2017. Before that, the topic was addressed as part of Building Block 1, devoted to the objective of the international framework, and Building Block 4, dedicated to its principles.

During early debates, the extent of the 'due regard' obligation was questioned, with some members asking for more substantive language. Nevertheless, the Working Group decided not to lay down a detailed definition of the 'due regard' principle as this would have exceeded the scope of its mandate. In fact, since Building Block 9 mirrors Article IX OST, which is a fundamental provision of international space law, the Working Group considered that the meaning of 'due regard' should derive from this provision, and not vice-versa.

Further comments concerned the need to specifically address the interests of developing and pioneer countries, as well as criticism raised against the mention of humankind

14 The M/V 'Norstar' case, Panama v. Italy, 10 April 2019, par. 199 ff.

alongside all countries. As to the first proposal, it was decided to specifically consider the interests of developing and pioneer countries in Building Blocks 4 and 13. As to the criticism against the mention of humankind alongside all countries, the Working Group decided to maintain both terms in order to reflect the contemporary architecture of the global society, which is no longer composed solely of sovereign States but also of governmental and non-governmental entities representing the many facets of humankind.

The Socio-Economic Panel presents an argument for considering a concept from the terrestrial mining sector – the 'Social License to Operate' – in the context of Building Block 9. While the term 'due regard' has a legal dimension, which the Socio-Economic Panel has not attempted to address, it is also believed to have relevant policy and market interaction aspects. The term 'Social License to Operate' (SLO) generally refers to efforts and activities an extractive company takes to building and maintaining goodwill or social capital with the communities affected by the operations of the company. As such, common elements addressed through SLO activities can help to identify and describe benefits arising from extractive activities and the ways in which operators interact with stakeholders to address negative impacts. It considers environmental impact, cultural and heritage impacts, monetary and non-monetary benefits, and supply chain affects, among other topics. However, SLO has been criticized in some instances as a loosely-defined concept that allows companies to market or describe activities positively, with little depth of implementation. Nonetheless, the Socio-Economic Panel considers reference to SLO to be instructive for the analysis of Building Block 9, as an example of how terrestrial extractive industry operators give due regard to the interests of the stakeholders affected by their operations (See Annex III).

Through those debates, the Working Group ultimately reached consensus on the final version of this Building Block at the face-to-face meeting of April 2019.

10 Avoidance and Mitigation of Potentially Harmful Impacts Resulting from Space Resource Activities

1 Text

Taking into account the current state of technology, the international framework should provide that States and international organizations responsible for space resource activities shall adopt appropriate measures with the aim of avoiding and mitigating potentially harmful impacts, including:

a. **Risks to the safety of persons, the environment or property;**
b. **Damage to persons, the environment or property;**

c. **Adverse changes in the environment of the Earth, taking into account internationally agreed planetary protection policies;**
d. **Harmful contamination of celestial bodies, taking into account internationally agreed planetary protection policies;**
e. **Harmful contamination of outer space;**
f. **Harmful effects of the creation of space debris;**
g. **Harmful interference with other on-going space activities, including other space resource activities;**
h. **Changes to designated and internationally endorsed outer space natural or cultural heritage sites;**
i. **Adverse changes to designated and internationally endorsed outer space sites of scientific interest.**

2 Explanation

Building Block 10 contemplates proactive measures to be adopted by States and international organizations to avoid and mitigate any potentially harmful impacts emerging from space resource activities. The long-term sustainability of space resource activities is therefore aimed at, through different courses of action, reflecting current concerns and acknowledging scientific progress. In doing so, it is suggested that the international framework must take into account the current state of technology, which might affect the means and alternatives available for conducting the measures indicated.

Due to their technical complexity, space resource activities undoubtedly pose a significant risk of harm and, like other space activities, should be perceived as ultra-hazardous, therefore demanding a high standard of care and proper due diligence. In this context, Building Block 10, taking into account the current state of technology, indicates that States and international organizations responsible for space resource activities shall adopt appropriate measures with the aim of avoiding and mitigating potentially harmful impacts, in accordance with the international framework.

According to Article VI OST, States bear international responsibility for national activities, irrespective of whether they are carried out by governmental or non-governmental entities. In this context, states shall authorize activities of non-governmental entities in outer space and ensure that they are carried out in conformity with international space law. However, both content of an authorization and subsequent supervision are left to the discretion of States. Article VI OST is therefore understood as the basis for national space legislation. Since non-governmental entities are not bound by the OST, Building Block 10 aims to adequately equip national authorities with effectives tools in order to address potentially harmful impacts resulting from space resource activities carried out by non-governmental entities at the national level.

An explanatory and non-exhaustive list of potentially harmful impacts to be considered for proper avoidance and mitigation is presented in subparagraphs (a) to (i) of Building Block 10, accounting for a total of nine instances.

First, reference is made to risk to the safety of persons, the environment or property (subparagraph (a)), followed by damage to persons, the environment or property (subparagraph (b)). Next, adverse changes to the environment of the Earth (subparagraph (c)) and harmful contamination of celestial bodies are mentioned (subparagraph (d)), with specific reference to internationally agreed planetary protection policies, such as those developed and continuously updated by COSPAR (Committee on Space Research).[15]

Harmful contamination of outer space is then addressed (subparagraph (e)), followed by harmful effects of the creation of space debris (subparagraph (f)). Additionally, harmful interference with other space activities is listed, whether involving space resources or not (subparagraph (g)). According to the Technical Panel (see Annex II), the most likely harmful interference between space resource activities would be of a technical character Although interference between radio frequencies can be mitigated through the procedures developed by the ITU, other instances of technical interferences applicable to space resource activities should not be taken for granted.

Designated and internationally endorsed outer space natural or cultural heritage sites are of explicit concern, considering that could be established at some point (subparagraph (h)). As space resource activities mature, those sites may be subject to international mechanisms of accreditation, deserving proper measures against any undesirable change. The same is applicable to outer space sites of scientific interest (subparagraph (i)), understood as areas considered to best represent the natural heritage.

In order to support the implementation of Building Block 10, the Socio-Economic Panel formulated recommendations in a white paper titled 'Developing Responsible Investing Principles for Space Resources' (see Annex III). The Panel calls for consideration of consensus principles to guide responsible investing, banking, and financing of space resource activities. Such principles would help to integrate sustainability and ethics concepts into the management of the space resources sector. Principles of this type exist in several terrestrial industry and finance segments, as identified by the Panel, which recommends considering and adapting such precedents to apply to space resources development. These principles could also potentially serve as an informing factor for the future development of industry operator focused best practices and/or standards – once the space resources industry matures to a point in which these become relevant.

---

15 Available at: https://cosparhq.cnes.fr/assets/uploads/2019/12/PPPolicyDecember-2017.pdf, accessed and verified on 20 December 2019.

The Socio-Economic Panel suggests consideration of the concept of Social License to Operate (SLO) from the terrestrial mining sector as a relevant concept for Building Block 9. SLO is also deemed relevant for Building Block 10. SLO generally refers to efforts and activities an extractive company takes to building and maintain goodwill or social capital with the communities close to where they operate. This goodwill is generated by activities to ensure the affected community benefits (monetarily or non-monetarily) as a result of the extractive operations. SLO can additionally address efforts to mitigate harmful or negative impacts of operations.

3 Legal Basis

Article IX OST introduced general considerations on the protection of the outer space environment, taking into account the possible negative effects of space activities. By promoting cooperation and mutual assistance between States acting on outer space, the provision introduces a legal foundation for avoidance and mitigation of harmful effects, although the wording reflects the international concerns that prevailed during the time of adoption:

> In the exploration and use of outer space, including the Moon and other celestial bodies, States Parties to the Treaty shall be guided by the principle of cooperation and mutual assistance and shall conduct all their activities in outer space, including the Moon and other celestial bodies, with due regard to the corresponding interests of all other States Parties to the Treaty. States Parties to the Treaty shall pursue studies of outer space, including the Moon and other celestial bodies, and conduct exploration of them so as to avoid their harmful contamination and also adverse changes in the environment of the Earth resulting from the introduction of extraterrestrial matter and, where necessary, shall adopt appropriate measures for this purpose. If a State Party to the Treaty has reason to believe that an activity or experiment planned by it or its nationals in outer space, including the Moon and other celestial bodies, would cause potentially harmful interference with activities of other States Parties in the peaceful exploration and use of outer space, including the Moon and other celestial bodies, it shall undertake appropriate international consultations before proceeding with any such activity or experiment. A State Party to the Treaty which has reason to believe that an activity or experiment planned by another State Party in outer space, including the Moon and other celestial bodies, would cause potentially harmful interference with activities in the peaceful exploration

> and use of outer space, including the Moon and other celestial bodies, may request consultation concerning the activity or experiment.

Article IX OST was based on paragraph 6 of the Declaration of Legal Principles, which provides:

> In the exploration and use of outer space, States shall be guided by the principle of cooperation and mutual assistance and shall conduct all their activities in outer space with due regard for the corresponding interests of other States. If a State has reason to believe that an outer space activity or experiment planned by it or its nationals would cause potentially harmful interference with activities of other States in the peaceful exploration and use of outer space, it shall undertake appropriate international consultations before proceeding with any such activity or experiment. A State which has reason to believe that an outer space activity or experiment planned by another State would cause potentially harmful interference with activities in the peaceful exploration and use of outer space may request consultation concerning the activity or experiment.

For the States Parties to the MA, said treaty follows the same rationale by focusing on balance of the environment of celestial bodies in its Article 7, paragraph 1:

> In exploring and using the Moon, States Parties shall take measures to prevent the disruption of the existing balance of its environment, whether by introducing adverse changes in that environment, by its harmful contamination through the introduction of extra-environmental matter or otherwise. States Parties shall also take measures to avoid harmfully affecting the environment of the Earth through the introduction of extraterrestrial matter or otherwise.

Paragraph 2 of Article 7 MA supports publicity of measures mentioned in the preceding paragraph, while introducing considerations in relation to radioactive materials:

> States Parties shall inform the Secretary-General of the United Nations of the measures being adopted by them in accordance with paragraph 1 of this article and shall also, to the maximum extent feasible, notify him in advance of all placements by them of radioactive materials on the Moon and of the purposes of such placements.

Finally, the last paragraph of Article 7 MA is devoted to areas of scientific interest that may be designated as international scientific preserves:

> States Parties shall report to other States Parties and to the Secretary General concerning areas of the Moon having special scientific interest in order that, without prejudice to the rights of other States Parties, consideration may be given to the designation of such areas as international scientific preserves for which special protective arrangements are to be agreed upon in consultation with the competent bodies of the United Nations.

The MA also mentions in Article 4, paragraph 1, that:

> Due regard shall be paid to the interests of present and future generations as well as to the need to promote higher standards of living and conditions of economic and social progress and development in accordance with the Charter of the United Nations.

Regarding the safety of persons, Article 10, paragraph 1 MA provides that:

> States shall adopt all practicable measures to safeguard life and health of persons on the Moon. For this purpose, they shall regard any person on the Moon as an astronaut within the meaning of Article V of the Treaty on Principles Governing the Activities of States in the Exploration and Use of Space, including the Moon and other Celestial Bodies and as part of the personnel of a spacecraft within the meaning of the Agreement on the Rescue of Astronauts, the Return of Astronauts and the Return of Objects Launched into Outer Space.

4 Alternatives Discussed

Mitigation of harmful impacts related to space resource activities was addressed by a single Building Block since the Working Group's first meeting in April 2016. However, numerous changes in wording and scope occurred during the drafting process. Even the title changed several times: 'Prevention and mitigation of harmful impact of outer space activities' was the one in the April 2016 meeting, being replaced by 'Prevention abatement of harmful impacts of outer space activities' in November 2016 and, finally, by 'Avoidance of harmful impacts resulting from space resource activities', as agreed in April 2017. The final version of Building Block 10 was agreed in the Working Group meeting of April 2019.

Regarding the scope of Building Block 10, especially its list of examples, it originally addressed only the following items: changes to designated and internationally endorsed outer space heritage sites; harmful contamination of celestial bodies; and adverse changes in the environment of the Earth. The revised text following the November 2016 meeting included adverse changes to sites of scientific interest, damage to persons, the environment or property, and mitigation of space debris. As a result of the April 2017 meeting, further additions introduced risk to the safety of persons, the environment or property, adverse changes in the natural condition of celestial bodies, and harmful interference with the normal operations of other on-going space activities.

Until November 2018, the Building Block required 'adoption of a precautionary approach with the aim of avoiding harmful impacts.' However, during the final stage of the drafting process, reference to the precautionary approach was removed.

During the meeting of November 2019, it was expressed that the avoidance of harmful impact as requirement for the lawful conduct of space resource activities does not reflect the relevant provisions of the Outer Space Treaty and the ITU Regulations. Article IX OST calls for States to engage in consultations, should they foresee that one of their activities may cause harmful interference with the activity of another State. Article 45 of the ITU Constitution calls for refraining from harmful interference to radio services by abiding to the ITU Radio Regulations, whereas Article 48 excludes certain activities, namely military radio installations, from the ITU regime. It was viewed that, if the international framework required States to take measures to avoid and mitigate potentially harmful interference, Building Block 10 would go beyond the scope of the aforementioned regulations.

Outer space natural or cultural heritage sites and outer space sites of scientific interest were often discussed during the meetings. Although there are currently no endorsed sites nor international mechanism to establish them, the matter of avoiding harmful impact caused by space resource activities with such sites was considered sufficiently important to be included in the final version of Building Block 10, as agreed in April 2019.

11 Technical Standards for, Prior Review of, and Safety Zones Around Space Resource Activities

1 Text

11.1 The international framework should provide that States and international organizations shall require the conduct of a review prior to a decision to proceed with a space resource activity to ascertain that such an activity is carried out in a safe manner to avoid harmful impacts.

11.2 The international framework should encourage the development of:

a. **Procedures to ensure that equipment, operational procedures, and processes applied in space resource activities avoid harmful impacts;**

b. **Methodology to assess that equipment, operational procedures, and processes applied in space resource activities meet common technical standards (conformity assessment);**
c. **Technical standards for equipment, operational procedures, and processes applied in space resource activities (standardization).**

11.3 Taking into account the principle of non-appropriation under Article II OST, the international framework should permit States and international organizations responsible for space resource activities to establish a safety zone, or other area-based safety measure, around an area identified for a space resource activity as necessary to assure safety and to avoid any harmful interference with that space resource activity. Such safety measure shall not impede the free access, in accordance with international law, to any area of outer space by personnel, vehicles and equipment of another operator. In accordance with the area-based safety measure, a State or international organization may restrict access for a limited period of time, provided that timely public notice has been given setting out the reasons for such restriction.

11.4 The international framework should provide that appropriate international consultations are undertaken in case of possible overlap of safety zones or conflicts involving the freedom of access recognized by international law.

2 *Explanation*

Building Block 11 acknowledges the inherent risks of space resource activities, recalling principles of international space law. To address those concerns, safety zones around space resource activities and interrelated issues are covered in four paragraphs. The first asserts that in order to avoid harmful impacts of space resource activities, States and international organizations must carry out a review prior to any decision to proceed with a space resource activity (paragraph 11.1). Therefore, a due regard procedure should be provided for in the international framework, in order to safeguard that the space resource activity in question is conducted safely.

Due to its subject matter, there is a connection with Building Block 5 on international responsibility for space resource activities, with Building Block 10 on the avoidance and mitigation of potentially harmful impacts resulting from space resource activities, and with Building Block 12 regarding monitoring and redressing of harmful impacts resulting therefrom. Safety zones are different from priority rights, which are addressed in Building Block 7 (access to space resources) and Building Block 14 (registration and sharing of information).

Initiatives for the international framework are subsequently suggested in paragraph 11.2, to address the concerns listed in the previous clause, in order to enhance transparency and international cooperation. Thus, certain actions are encouraged in three subparagraphs, the first of which concerns the development of procedures to be conducted prior, after or independently from the space resource activity, to ensure that equipment, operational procedures and processes applied therein avoid harmful impacts (subparagraph (a)). Second, the development of a conformity assessment is suggested in order to verify that equipment, operational procedures and processes applied to space resource activities meet common technical standards (subparagraph (b)). Finally, standardization is proposed in relation to equipment, operational procedures and processes (subparagraph (c)). In this regard, one should recognize the importance of standardization bodies, *i.e.*, public or private, domestic or international, organizations that propose, develop, establish, monitor and coordinate voluntary standards, designed to address the needs and technical requirements of a certain activity. Common technical standards (standardization) are important accelerators for the exploration and utilization of outer space contributing to the long-term sustainability of outer space.[16]

Safety zones or other area-based safety measures are addressed in paragraph 11.3. They are to be created around an area identified as necessary to ensure safety for a space resource activity and to avoid possible harmful interference. Based on duly motivated prior public notice, access may be restricted in accordance with the area-based safety measure for a limited period of time. However, any decision to establish a safety zone should cautiously balance the need to ensure safety and the principle of non-appropriation, as well as the freedom of access to all areas of celestial bodies, both of which are enshrined in the OST. Granting free access to other operators is therefore to be considered by the international framework in relation to any area of outer space, and applicable to personnel, vehicles and equipment.

International disagreement may emerge in relation to different aspects of safety zones, which might cover considerably larger areas than the exploitation zone, since different factors could harmfully impact the safety of space resource activities in the vicinity. Certainly, the entry into safety zones by third parties which causes damage to operators would entail international responsibility in accordance with international law. In case of overlap of safety zones or conflicts involving freedom of access, paragraph 11.4 suggests appropriate international consultations to be implemented and provided by the international framework.

16 For instance, the Lunar Ore Reserve Standards (LORS-101), is a collaborative effort designed to serve as a first code for the reporting of lunar exploration results, lunar resources, and lunar reserves. The classification framework considers geological uncertainty, project and technology maturity, together with socio-political and economic viability. LORS-101 also includes a glossary for SRU and makes a comparison to similar definitions currently used in the Oil & Gas and Mining Industry. *See*: https://az659834.vo.msecnd.net/eventsairseasiaprod/production-ausimm-public/72db098c56a74b9d8a5adbfab58b389e (accessed and verified on 20 December 2019).

The Technical Panel considered the topic of safety zones in one of its teams, recognizing the importance of additional coordination to avoid harmful interference. The following five principles were proposed in that regard:

1. Safety zones should be established, maintained, and terminated in a manner that protects public and private personnel, equipment, and operations from harmful interference;
2. Safety zones shall be established, maintained, and terminated in a manner that fully complies with the Outer Space Treaty;
3. Safety zones should be established by determining the area in which nominal operations of the relevant activity or an anomalous event could reasonably cause harmful interference with other parties' personnel, equipment, or operations;
4. The entity establishing, maintaining, or terminating a safety zone shall be able to publicly provide the basis for the zone to the extent practicable without violating national export control laws or the confidentiality of commercial information and/or intellectual property; and
5. Safety zones shall be utilized in a manner that encourages the robust, safe, and efficient extraction and utilization of space resources.

The final report of the Technical Panel team responsible for safety zones on the Moon and asteroids, including pertinent discussions and conclusions, is included herein as Annex II.

3 Legal Basis

The establishment of technical standards and proper prior review of safety zones is linked to the international provisions related to international responsibility for national space activities. In accordance with Article VI OST, States Parties shall bear international responsibility for national activities in outer space, whether are carried on by governmental agencies or by non-governmental entities, and for assuring conformity with the applicable legal provisions. In addition, activities of non-governmental entities in outer space should be authorized and continuously supervised by the appropriate State Party:

> States Parties to the Treaty shall bear international responsibility for national activities in outer space, including the Moon and other celestial bodies, whether such activities are carried on by governmental agencies or by non-governmental entities, and for assuring that national activities are carried out in conformity with the provisions set forth in the present Treaty. The activities of

> non-governmental entities in outer space, including the Moon and other celestial bodies, shall require authorization and continuing supervision by the appropriate State Party to the Treaty. When activities are carried on in outer space, including the Moon and other celestial bodies, by an international organization, responsibility for compliance with this Treaty shall be borne both by the international organization and by the States Parties to the Treaty participating in such organization.

For the States Parties to the MA, similar responsibility provisions are identified therein, as described in its Article 14, paragraph 1 and further elaborated above.

These Articles codified the principle established by paragraph 5 Declaration of Legal Principles:

> States bear international responsibility for national activities in outer space, whether carried on by governmental agencies or by non-governmental entities, and for assuring that national activities are carried on in conformity with the principles set forth in the present Declaration. The activities of non-governmental entities in outer space shall require authorization and continuing supervision by the State concerned. When activities are carried on in outer space by an international organization, responsibility for compliance with the principles set forth in this Declaration shall be borne by the international organization and by the States participating in it.

As far as harmful impacts related to space resource activities are concerned, legal basis may be found in Article IX OST, which does not distinguish between intentional and unintentional interference:

> In the exploration and use of outer space, including the Moon and other celestial bodies, States Parties to the Treaty shall be guided by the principle of cooperation and mutual assistance and shall conduct all their activities in outer space, including the Moon and other celestial bodies, with due regard to the corresponding interests of all other States Parties to the Treaty. States Parties to the Treaty shall pursue studies of outer space, including the Moon and other celestial bodies, and conduct exploration of them so as to avoid their harmful contamination and also adverse changes in the environment of the Earth resulting from the introduction of extraterrestrial matter and, where necessary, shall adopt appropriate measures for this purpose. If a State Party to the Treaty has reason to believe that an activity or experiment planned by it or its nationals in outer space, including the Moon and other celestial bodies, would cause

> potentially harmful interference with activities of other States Parties in the peaceful exploration and use of outer space, including the Moon and other celestial bodies, it shall undertake appropriate international consultations before proceeding with any such activity or experiment. A State Party to the Treaty which has reason to believe that an activity or experiment planned by another State Party in outer space, including the Moon and other celestial bodies, would cause potentially harmful interference with activities in the peaceful exploration and use of outer space, including the Moon and other celestial bodies, may request consultation concerning the activity or experiment.

Likewise, Article 4 MA calls, in paragraph 1, for due regard to the interests of present and future generations and, in paragraph 2, for the cooperation and mutual assistance among States. Furthermore, Article 7, paragraph 1 MA provides for the prevention of disruption of the existing balance of the Moon.

Paragraph 6 of the Declaration of Legal Principles, included the same principle:

> In the exploration and use of outer space, States shall be guided by the principle of cooperation and mutual assistance and shall conduct all their activities in outer space with due regard for the corresponding interests of other States. If a State has reason to believe that an outer space activity or experiment planned by it or its nationals would cause potentially harmful interference with activities of other States in the peaceful exploration and use of outer space, it shall undertake appropriate international consultations before proceeding with any such activity or experiment. A State which has reason to believe that an outer space activity or experiment planned by another State would cause potentially harmful interference with activities in the peaceful exploration and use of outer space may request consultation concerning the activity or experiment.

Finally, paragraph 11.3 of Building Block 11 includes specific reference to Article II OST, which codified the principle of non-appropriation:

> Outer space, including the Moon and other celestial bodies, is not subject to national appropriation by claim of sovereignty, by means of use or occupation, or by any other means.

The referred principle was covered by the United Nations General Assembly Resolutions Resolution 1721 A (XVI), of 1961, and 1962 (XVIII), 1963. In accordance with paragraph 3 of the later instrument:

> Outer space and celestial bodies are not subject to national appropriation by claim of sovereignty, by means of use or occupation, or by any other means.

The Moon Agreement also included this principle in Article 11, paragraph 2:

> The Moon is not subject to national appropriation by any claim of sovereignty, by means of use or occupation, or by any other means.[17]

4 *Alternatives Discussed*

Since the first face-to-face meeting in 2016, the Working Group reserved one of the Building Blocks to deal with safety of space resource activities. In fact, until April 2017, current Building Block 10 was simply titled 'Safety of space resource activities'. Its scope was extended in 2017 when a paragraph dealing with technical standards was added. The fourth paragraph addressing possible overlap of safety zones or conflicts with the freedom of access was added during the meeting of April 2019.

Significant attention was devoted to safety zones. During the meetings, there were many discussions as to the compatibility of safety zones with the principles of international space law, particularly the non-appropriation principle and the freedom of access to all areas of celestial bodies.

During the final session of November 2019, the final wording was agreed by the Working Group, clarifying its content.

12 Monitoring and Redressing Harmful Impacts Resulting from Space Resource Activities

1 *Text*

12.1 The international framework should provide that States and international organizations shall ensure monitoring of any harmful impacts resulting from space resource activities for which they are responsible.

12.2 If a harmful impact resulting from a space resource activity occurs, or is reasonably expected to occur, the international framework should provide that the State or international organization responsible for the space resource activity shall implement

17 In accordance with Article 1, Paragraph 2, for the purposes of the Moon Agreement 'reference to the Moon shall include orbits around or other trajectories to or around it.'

measures to respond to such harmful impact (response measures) and consider whether the space resource activity should be adjusted or terminated (adaptive management).

2 *Explanation*

Building Block 12 aims to reduce risks resulting from space resource activities and to promote long-term sustainability of outer space activities. Due to potentially harmful impacts resulting from space resource activities, States and international organizations shall ensure effective monitoring of the activities which they authorized.

Building Block 12 must be read in close connection with Building Block 10 on the avoidance and mitigation of potentially harmful impacts. The measures mentioned in the title are addressed in two interrelated paragraphs in order to provide further clarification.

Paragraph 12.1 considers the act, by States and international organizations responsible for space resource activities, of monitoring any possible harmful impact resulting from them. If such harmful impact materializes, or can reasonably be expected of doing so, paragraph 12.2 suggests that the international framework should consider appropriate responsive measures.

Paragraph 12.2 goes a step further by requiring the State or international organization responsible for space resource activities which caused, or is reasonably expected to cause, harmful impacts, to consider if the activity in question should be adjusted or even terminated. Such appraisal, which would certainly result in vast implications, is to be based on the principle of adaptive management, *i.e.*, a decision-making process aimed at adjusting behavior and decision-making based on experience and actual changes. In order to fulfil their international obligations, States and international organizations should promote robust and effective national space legislation providing them with necessary means for acting in case of non-conformity.

What should be considered as harmful impact, as far as space resource activities are concerned, depends on actual and specific circumstances, to be further appraised at a later stage. Nevertheless biocontamination, understood as contamination with biological material or agents, as well as other forms of deleterious contagion, should be taken into consideration by the international framework, in accordance with the reasoning contained in Building Block 12.

3 *Legal Basis*

The applicable legal basis for Building Block 12 may be found, alike Building Block 10, on Article IX OST:

> In the exploration and use of outer space, including the Moon and other celestial bodies, States Parties to the Treaty shall be guided by the principle of cooperation and mutual assistance and shall conduct all their activities in outer space, including the Moon and other celestial bodies, with due regard to the corresponding interests of all other States Parties to the Treaty. States Parties to the Treaty shall pursue studies of outer space, including the Moon and other celestial bodies, and conduct exploration of them so as to avoid their harmful contamination and also adverse changes in the environment of the Earth resulting from the introduction of extraterrestrial matter and, where necessary, shall adopt appropriate measures for this purpose. If a State Party to the Treaty has reason to believe that an activity or experiment planned by it or its nationals in outer space, including the Moon and other celestial bodies, would cause potentially harmful interference with activities of other States Parties in the peaceful exploration and use of outer space, including the Moon and other celestial bodies, it shall undertake appropriate international consultations before proceeding with any such activity or experiment. A State Party to the Treaty which has reason to believe that an activity or experiment planned by another State Party in outer space, including the Moon and other celestial bodies, would cause potentially harmful interference with activities in the peaceful exploration and use of outer space, including the Moon and other celestial bodies, may request consultation concerning the activity or experiment.

For the States Parties to the MA, due regard to the interests of present and future generations is envisioned in Article 4, paragraph 1. Additionally, Article 7, paragraph 1 MA includes provisions regarding the protection of the lunar environment:

> In exploring and using the Moon, States Parties shall take measures to prevent the disruption of the existing balance of its environment, whether by introducing adverse changes in that environment, by its harmful contamination through the introduction of extra-environmental matter or otherwise. States Parties shall also take measures to avoid harmfully affecting the environment of the Earth through the introduction of extraterrestrial matter or otherwise.

Paragraph 2 of Article 7 MA reads:

> States Parties shall inform the Secretary-general of the United Nations of the measures being adopted by them in accordance with paragraph 1 of this article and shall also, to the maximum extent feasible, notify him in advance of all

> placements by them of radioactive materials on the moon and of the purpose of such placements.

Moreover, regarding interference with the activities of another State, according to Article 8, paragraph 3 MA:

> Activities of States Parties in accordance with paragraphs 1 and of this article shall not interfere with the activities of other States Parties on the Moon. Where such interference may occur, the States Parties concerned shall undertake consultations in accordance with article 15, paragraphs 2 and 3, of this Agreement.

More specifically on interference, Article 5, paragraph 2 MA establishes that:

> If a State Party becomes aware that another State Party plans to operate simultaneously in the same area of or in the same orbit or trajectory to or around the Moon, it shall promptly inform the other State of the timing of and plans for its own operations.

The referred provisions are based on the principle established by paragraph 6 of the Declaration of Legal Principles:

> In the exploration and use of outer space, States shall be guided by the principle of cooperation and mutual assistance and shall conduct all their activities in outer space with due regard for the corresponding interests of other States. If a State has reason to believe that an outer space activity or experiment planned by it or its nationals would cause potentially harmful interference with activities of other States in the peaceful exploration and use of outer space, it shall undertake appropriate international consultations before proceeding with any such activity or experiment. A State which has reason to believe that an outer space activity or experiment planned by another State would cause potentially harmful interference with activities in the peaceful exploration and use of outer space may request consultation concerning the activity or experiment.

The territorial scope contained in the current Building Block can may be found in Article 1, paragraph 1 MA, which reads:

> The provisions of this Agreement relating to the Moon shall also apply to other celestial bodies within the solar system, other than the Earth, except insofar as specific legal norms enter into force with respect to any of these celestial bodies.

4 *Alternatives Discussed*

Originally, the Building Block was dedicated only to monitoring and inspection of space resource activities. It also provided that States and international organizations should report on the space resource activities authorized by them. However, reference to an obligation to report was removed in November 2016. In April 2017, the inspection of space resource activities became the topic of a new Building Block, Building Block 17, and this Building Block was renamed 'Monitoring and redressing harmful impact resulting from space resource activities' after the meeting of September 2017. The final version of Building Block 12 was agreed in April 2019.

13 Sharing of Benefits Arising out of the Utilization of Space Resources

1 *Text*

13.1 Bearing in mind that the exploration and use of outer space shall be carried out for the benefit and in the interests of all countries and humankind, the international framework should provide that States and international organizations responsible for space resource activities shall provide for benefit-sharing through the promotion of the participation in space resource activities by all countries, in particular developing countries. Benefits may include, but not be limited to enabling, facilitating, promoting and fostering:

a. **The development of space science and technology and of its applications;**
b. **The development of relevant and appropriate capabilities in interested States;**
c. **Cooperation and contribution in education and training;**
d. **Access to and exchange of information;**
e. **Incentivization of joint ventures;**
f. **The exchange of expertise and technology among States on a mutually acceptable basis;**
g. **The establishment of an international fund.**

13.2 The international framework should not require compulsory monetary benefit-sharing.
13.3 Operators should be encouraged to provide for benefit-sharing.

2 *Explanation*

Benefit-sharing, to be promoted by States and international organizations responsible for space resource activities, is addressed in Building Block 13 through the advancement of participation by all countries, in particular developing nations. This provision is meant to implement Article I OST, ensuring that space resource activities will be beneficial for all countries and humankind. By contemplating an inclusive perspective, Building Block 13 emphasizes the global nature of space and its inherent tendency to openness and cooperation.

The reasoning for this provision lies in the acknowledgement that, in accordance with international law, the exploration and use of outer space, including the Moon and other celestial bodies, shall be carried out for the benefit and in the interests of all countries, and of humankind as a whole. Taking into consideration the wide-ranging effects expected to emerge from space resource activities, the channeling of benefits to the international community should be ensured by the applicable international framework. Accordingly, Building Block 13 suggests that the international framework shall ensure the inclusiveness of space resource activities.

Since there are many different ways in which outer space is being used, there can be various mechanisms to share benefits. From this perspective, Building Block 13 provides a non-exhaustive list of examples, most of which have already been successfully adopted in the space industry, to be assessed by States and international organizations responsible for space resource activities. The proposed means were devised as inclusive initiatives, based on shared values, and capable of fostering effective results. Thus, the perspectives of developing and emerging space faring nations, as far as space resource activities are concerned, were properly taken into account. At the same time, Building Block 13 seeks to ensure benefit sharing through instruments that do not threaten the commercial aspect of space resource activities, which are fundamental to sustain the development of the industry in the first place.

The first method of benefit sharing is the development of space science and technology and their applications (subparagraph (a)), followed by the development of relevant and appropriate capabilities in interested States (subparagraph (b)). Also, cooperation and contribution in education and training is suggested (subparagraph (c)), along with access to and exchange of information (subparagraph (d)). The incentivization of joint ventures, integrating different nations from around the globe in space resource activities, is introduced as a relevant possibility (subparagraph (e)). Reference is further made to the exchange of technology and expertise, on a mutually acceptable basis and necessarily in accordance with, and within the limits of, applicable domestic regulations (subparagraph (f)). Finally, the establishment of an international fund, to be provided by States, is mentioned as another option to be opportunely considered (subparagraph (g)).

Building Block 13 calls for sharing of benefits arising out of the utilization of space resources with an emphasis on non-monetary benefits, as indicated in paragraph 13.2. Additionally, paragraph 13.3 foresees a direct role also for operators, insofar as it envisages the development of appropriate incentives for them to engage in benefit-sharing.

A fundamental assumption that is made in many of the suggested benefit types enumerated herein is increased participation in aspects of space resource activities by actors in States that are not among the leading spacefaring nations. Accordingly, the Socio-Economic Panel provides further input for the development of space resources related capacity building programs, as an element of the implementation strategy for Building Block 13.

To achieve the benefit sharing models listed therein, the Socio-Economic Panel suggests that capacity building models need to consider two audiences/stakeholder groups: a) those who do not yet have access or an understanding about what is happening in the space resources sector and b) arena, and/or those who are aware, to a greater or lesser degree, on what is happening but are isolated by their decision-makers.

The overall goal of capacity building related to space resource activities should be to facilitate access to, and exchange of, the knowledge and outcomes produced by space resource activities. Capacity building activities of this type will expedite the development of an international framework on space resource activities. The full report of the Socio-Economic Panel regarding recommendations on 'Capacity Building Programs for Benefiting from the Exploration and Utilization of Space Resources' is included as Annex III.

3 Legal Basis

International law support for Building Block 13 may identified in Article 1, paragraph 1, OST:

> The exploration and use of outer space, including the Moon and other celestial bodies, shall be carried out for the benefit and in the interests of all countries, irrespective of their degree of economic or scientific development, and shall be the province of all mankind.

Article I OST is often referred to as the cornerstone of the entire system of international space law, since it lays down the very essential rules related to the exploration and use of outer space. In particular, its first paragraph lays down two fundamental principles: the freedom to explore and use outer space, and its inherent global relevance. Accordingly, while each State is entitled to freely explore and use outer space, it should also exercise this freedom bearing in mind the interest of all countries and in a way that can be beneficial to them.

Building Block 13 brings this obligation even further, insofar as it also mentions 'humankind' alongside 'all countries'. The Working Group has elaborated this distinction in order to reflect the contemporary architecture of the global society, which is no longer composed solely by sovereign States but also of governmental and non-governmental entities, representing the many facets of humankind.

These provisions closely followed the principle endorsed by paragraph 1 Declaration of Legal Principles:

> The exploration and use of outer space shall be carried on for the benefit and in the interests of all mankind.

For the States Parties to the MA, similar language is included in its Article 4, paragraph 1:

> The exploration and use of the Moon shall be the province of all mankind and shall be carried out for the benefit and in the interests of all countries, irrespective of their degree of economic or scientific development. Due regard shall be paid to the interests of present and future generations as well as to the need to promote higher standards of living and conditions of economic and social progress and development in accordance with the Charter of the United Nations.

Additionally, paragraph 5 of Article 11 MA states that a legal regime to govern the exploitation of natural resources of the Moon (and consequently, in accordance with the treaty, other celestial bodies) shall be established by the States Parties as such exploitation is about to become feasible. The main purposes of the mentioned regime are developed by paragraph 7 of the same Article, which, in its letter d, includes:

> An equitable sharing by all States Parties in the benefits derived from those resources, whereby the interests and needs of the developing countries, as well as the efforts of those countries which have contributed either directly or indirectly to the exploration of the Moon, shall be given special consideration.

Finally, the United Nations General Assembly Resolution 51/122, of 1996, titled Declaration on International Cooperation in the Exploration and Use of Outer Space for the Benefit and in the Interest of All States, Taking into Particular Account the Needs of Developing Countries, includes, as paragraphs 1 and 3, the following texts:

> International cooperation in the exploration and use of outer space for peaceful purposes (hereafter 'international cooperation') shall be conducted in accordance with the provisions of international law, including the Charter of the United Nations and the Treaty on the Principles Governing the Activities of States in the Exploration and Use of Outer Space, including the Moon and Other Celestial Bodies. It shall be carried out for the benefit and in the interest of all States, irrespective of their degree of economic, social or scientific and technological development, and shall be the province of all mankind. Particular account should be taken of the needs of developing countries.
> All States, particularly those with relevant space capabilities and with programmes for the exploration and use of outer space, should contribute to promoting and fostering international cooperation on an equitable and mutually acceptable basis. In this context, particular attention should be given to the benefit for and the interests of developing countries and countries with incipient space programmes stemming from such international cooperation conducted with countries with more advanced space capabilities.

4 *Alternatives Discussed*

The Building Block regarding benefit sharing was introduced for open discussion at the Working Group during its first face-to-face meeting in April 2016. Members and observers have thoroughly appraised, in detail, various perspectives involving this delicate topic, in order to find the best possible solution.

Through a thoughtful debate, the content and structure of Building Block 13 have evolved from the two original paragraphs to its current elaborated version, upon which the members have reached consensus during the face-to-face meeting of November 2018. For the most part, discussions focused on what could be the appropriate means for ensuring compliance with Article I OST, while not discouraging the industry from investing in space resource activities.

Inter alia, interventions within the Working Group showed significant support for the instrument provided by subparagraph (e), *i.e.* the promotion of joint ventures, considering that they could in fact enable all interested countries to directly participate, individually or collectively, in space resource activities. In this regard, the Working Group took into special consideration the 1996 'Declaration on International Cooperation in the Exploration and Use of Outer Space for the Benefit and Interest of All States, Taking into Particular Account the Needs of Developing Countries', adopted by the General Assembly of the United Nations with UNGA Resolution 51/122. Accordingly, it is the understanding of the Working Group that contractual terms in such cooperative ventures should be fair and reasonable and that they should be in full compliance with the legitimate rights and interests of the parties concerned, particularly with regard to export control limitation and intellectual property rights.

Another topical discussion saw the members and observers debating whether or not the international framework should require States to share revenues arising out of space resource activities. Ultimately, the Working Group decided not to include such provision, based on the premise that currently compulsory monetary sharing does not represent a suitable solution, due to the very early stage of space resource activities. It was also pointed out that in the short and medium term, the space resource activities of the operators are not expected to return sufficient or significant profit.

Rather, the Working Group favored the idea of an international fund, expressed in subparagraph (g), to be provided by States, which could be employed to support the mechanisms proposed in the previous subparagraphs. During the debates, different sources of funding were considered, as well as operational mechanisms and management alternatives, including providing information on potential contributors. Nevertheless, guided by the principle of adaptive governance, the Working Group decided not to link the international fund to any specific goal or funding source, since both these aspects could be better assessed once space resource activities have matured.

14 Registration and Sharing of Information

1 *Text*

The international framework should provide that States and international organizations shall:

a. **Register priority rights of an operator to search and/or recover space resources in accordance with the international framework;**
b. **Give advance notification of space resource activities, including any area-based safety measure associated with them, for which they are responsible through an international database;**
c. **Register space objects in accordance with the REG(i), United Nations General Assembly Resolution 1721 B (XVI)(ii), or Article XI OST, taking into account United Nations General Assembly Resolution 62/101(iii);**

d. **Notify frequency assignments for recording in the Master International Frequency Register in accordance with the Radio Regulations of the International Telecommunication Union;**
e. **Provide, taking into account Article XI OST and the legitimate interests of operators, information and best practices on the prior authorization and continuing supervision of space resource activities for which they are responsible through an international database, including:**
   i. **The purposes, locations, orbital parameters and duration of space resource activities;**
   ii. **The nature, conduct, and locations of space resource activities and associated logistic activities, for example deployment of stations, installations, equipment and vehicles;**
   iii. **The results of space resource activities;**
   iv. **Any phenomena discovered in outer space which could endanger terrestrial life or health, as well as of any indication of extraterrestrial life;**
   v. **Any harmful impacts resulting from space resource activities for which they are responsible and the measures planned or implemented to redress such impacts;**
f. **Notify the termination of space resource activities for which they are responsible through an international database together with a statement on the condition of the area where the space resource activity was carried out, including the presence of any space objects or space-made products, or parts thereof.**

(i) 1975 Convention on the Registration of Objects Launched into Outer Space.

(ii) 1961 Resolution 1721 B (XVI) adopted by the United Nations General Assembly, International Cooperation on the Peaceful Uses of Outer Space.

(iii) 2007 Resolution 62/101 adopted by the United Nations General Assembly, Recommendations on Enhancing the Practice of States and International Intergovernmental Organizations in Registering Space Objects.

2 *Explanation*

Building Block 14 considers appropriate registration and sharing of information, as far as space resource activities are concerned, through different mechanisms and actions, designed to foster transparency and confidence-building among operators, States and international organizations. This provision is meant to expand on Article XI OST, ensuring the highest possible degree of international cooperation in the utilization of space resources.

Because Building Block 14 is one of the final provisions, it needs to be read in conjunction with the other Building Blocks to which it explicitly or implicitly refers. Accordingly, this Building Block presents a rather complex structure, insofar as it addresses six different situations:

a. Registration of priority rights to search and/or recover space resources;
b. Advance notification of space resource activities, with particular focus on the eventual establishment of any area-based safety measures;
c. Registration of space objects involved in space resource activities;
d. Notification of frequency assignments for space resources missions;
e. Sharing of information and best practices on authorization and supervision of space resource activities; and
f. Notification of termination of space resource activities, with particular focus on the material consequences left behind in the area of interest.

Each part will be considered individually, followed by a final comment on their overall significance as part of Building Block 14.

Subparagraph (a) addresses registration of priority rights to search and/or recover space resources. It is connected with Building Block 7, which addresses 'Access to Space Resources' and provides for the attribution of the aforementioned priority rights.

Further, it is also connected with Building Block 18, subparagraph (a), which is dedicated to 'Institutional Arrangements' and provides for the establishment and maintenance of a 'publicly available international registry for registering priority rights'.

Thus, the purpose of subparagraph (a) of Building Block 14 is to mandate for the registration of the priority rights attributed under Building Block 7, within the international registry established under Building Block 18.

The rationale for subparagraph (a) stems from the necessity to avoid potential conflicting claims that could arise in the absence of an international registration procedure for priority rights to search and/or recover space resources.

Subparagraph (b) provides for the advance notification of space resource activities, with particular focus on the eventual establishment of any area-based safety measure associated with them. It is connected with Building Block 11, paragraph 11.3, which is dedicated to 'Technical Standards for, Prior Review of, and Safety Zones Around Space Resources Activities' and allows for the establishment of any area-based safety measure that is deemed to be necessary to ensure safety and to avoid any harmful interference with the relevant space resource activity.

Further, subparagraph (b) of Building Block 14 is connected also with Building Block 18, subparagraph (b), subparagraph (i), which is dedicated to 'Institutional Arrangements' and provides for the establishment and maintenance of an international database, in addition to the international registry, for making publicly available, *inter alia,* advance notifications of space resource activities.

Thus, the purpose of subparagraph (b) of Building Block 14 is to mandate for the advance notification of authorized space resource activities under Building Block 11, as well as of any area-based safety measures eventually related, within the international database established under Building Block 18. The rationale under consideration is to ensure awareness of all on-going space resource activities, in particular of their related area-based safety measures, in order to minimize the risk of harmful interference.

Subparagraph (c) of Building Block 14 deals with the registration of space objects in accordance with the applicable provisions of international space law, those being either the REG, UNGA Res. 1721B or Article XI OST, taking into account UNGA Res. 62/101, depending on the specific situation. Subparagraph (c) is not connected to any other Building Block and its purpose is to reinforce the applicability of general registration rules within the regulation of space resource activities.

Subparagraph (d) of Building Block 14 deals with the notification of frequency assignments for space resource activities in accordance with the ITU Radio Regulations. As such, it is not connected to any other Building Block and its rationale is to reinforce the applicability of general ITU rules within the regulation of space resource activities.

Subparagraph (e) of Building Block 14 provides for the sharing of information and best practices on the authorization and supervision of space resource activities among States and international organizations, taking into account Article XI OST and the legitimate interests of operators.

Subparagraph (e) is connected with Building Block 18, paragraph (b), subparagraph (i), which is dedicated to 'Institutional Arrangements' and provides for the establishment and maintenance of an international database, in addition to the international registry, for making publicly available, *inter alia,* all the relevant information about on-going missions.

The information requested under subparagraph (e) refers to the practical details of the relevant space resource activity, together with eventual phenomena discovered in outer space and harmful impacts resulting from the mission. Its justification is to foster the situational awareness of space resource activities through the collection of relevant information coming from on-going missions. Related requirements and specificities are to be considered by the relevant parties at the appropriate time.

Subparagraph (f) provides for the notification in relation to termination of space resource activities, together with a statement on the condition of the area where the mission was carried out, including the presence of any space objects or space products. It is linked with Building Block 18, subparagraph (b), subparagraph (i), which is dedicated to 'Institutional Arrangements' and provides for the establishment and maintenance of an international database, in addition to the international registry, for making publicly available, *inter alia,* all the relevant information about on-going missions.

The rationale for subparagraph (f) of Building Block 14 is to keep track of exhausted space resource activities, and most importantly of the consequences left behind in the area where each mission was carried out. The Technical Panel suggests that the international framework should clarify whether material left behind will continue to be owned by the operator that has conducted the space resource activity or whether it will become common property.

Overall, Building Block 14 has the purpose of enhancing transparency and confidence-building measures in the performance of space resource activities. Through a comprehensive set of requirements, Building Block 14 reinforces the applicability of existing instruments and further complements them with new practices that are specific to the utilization of space resources. Additionally, as one of the final provisions, Building Block 14 connects itself with others under the common umbrella of international cooperation.

3 Legal Basis

Because of its complex structure, Building Block 14 has more than one legal basis. Overall, it is based on Article XI OST, under which States Parties to the OST agree to provide the UN Secretary General with some basic information.

> In order to promote international cooperation in the peaceful exploration and use of outer space, States Parties to the Treaty conducting activities in outer space, including the Moon and other celestial bodies, agree to inform the Secretary-General of the United Nations as well as the public and the international scientific community, to the greatest extent feasible and practicable, of the nature, conduct, locations and the results of such activities. On receiving the said information, the Secretary-General of the United Nations should be prepared to disseminate it immediately and effectively.

For the States Parties to the MA, it provides for similar, yet more detailed, notification mechanism in its Article 5, paragraph 1:

> States Parties shall inform the Secretary-General of the United Nations as well as the public and the international scientific community, to the greatest extent feasible and practicable, of their activities concerned with the exploration and use of the Moon. Information on the time, purposes, locations, orbital parameters and duration shall be given in respect of each mission to the Moon

> as soon as possible after launching, while information on the results of each mission, including scientific results, shall be furnished upon completion of the mission. In the case of a mission lasting more than sixty days, information on conduct of the mission, including any scientific results, shall be given periodically, at thirty-day intervals. For missions lasting more than six months, only significant additions to such information need be reported thereafter.

Accordingly, Article IX OST embodies and re-states the idea of international cooperation in the exploration and use of space as a defining feature of the OST, as follows:

> In the exploration and use of outer space, including the Moon and other celestial bodies, States Parties to the Treaty shall be guided by the principle of cooperation and mutual assistance and shall conduct all their activities in outer space, including the Moon and other celestial bodies, with due regard to the corresponding interests of all other States Parties to the Treaty. States Parties to the Treaty shall pursue studies of outer space, including the Moon and other celestial bodies, and conduct exploration of them so as to avoid their harmful contamination and also adverse changes in the environment of the Earth resulting from the introduction of extraterrestrial matter and, where necessary, shall adopt appropriate measures for this purpose. If a State Party to the Treaty has reason to believe that an activity or experiment planned by it or its nationals in outer space, including the Moon and other celestial bodies, would cause potentially harmful interference with activities of other States Parties in the peaceful exploration and use of outer space, including the Moon and other celestial bodies, it shall undertake appropriate international consultations before proceeding with any such activity or experiment. A State Party to the Treaty which has reason to believe that an activity or experiment planned by another State Party in outer space, including the Moon and other celestial bodies, would cause potentially harmful interference with activities in the peaceful exploration and use of outer space, including the Moon and other celestial bodies, may request consultation concerning the activity or experiment.

Likewise, Article 4 MA reiterates in paragraph 2 the cooperation and mutual assistance among States, whereas Article 5, paragraph 2 calls for States to inform each other in case of conducting activities in the same area, orbit or trajectory.

As per the six parts of the Building Block, subparagraphs (a), (b), (e) and (f) are based on Article XI OST, while subparagraph (c) is further based on the REG, and subparagraph (d) relies on the ITU Constitution.

4 *Alternatives Discussed*

The Building Block regarding registration and sharing of information was introduced for open discussion at the Working Group during the face-to-face meeting of November 2016. As the Building Block evolved, the Working Group extended its scope until it has reached its present structure, upon which the members reached consensus in April 2019.

One of the main topics that has animated the debate on Building Block 14 concerned the entity which should be in charge of the registration process. First, a centralized international entity or a different mechanism, including national registries, were suggested. Ultimately, the Working Group decided to opt for a single entity in order to minimize the bureaucratic aspects.

Next, the Working Group considered whether to rely on existing UN Registers or to propose a new international register dedicated to space resource activities. Bearing in mind that both UNGA Resolution 1721/B and the REG deal exclusively with space *objects*, while the main subject of the international framework are *activities,* the Working Group opted for the establishment of a new international register.

Further to that, the debate among members and observers also showed that one international registry would not be enough to address all the different situations regulated under Building Block 14. Accordingly, the Working Group took the following two measures to address this issue.

First, it was agreed to maintain the *status quo* related to the registration of space objects (*i.e.* using REG, UNGA Res. 1721/B or Article XI OST, taking into account UNGA Res. 62/01) and the notification of frequency assignments (to be recorded in the Master International Frequency Register in accordance with the ITU Radio Regulations).

Second, the Working Group proposed to add an international database as a means to share certain relevant information without the typical formalities of an international registry. Thus, it was decided to limit the scope of the international registry to cover only the registration of priority rights and entrust the storage of the other information into the international database.

Another subject for discussion concerned the type of information that should be shared in the international database. In particular, some members proposed to restrict the scope of subparagraph (e) in order to protect commercially sensitive information. A view was expressed that Article XI OST does not entail an obligation to provide information, and therefore the required information for registration in subparagraph (e) should be deleted. Ultimately, consensus was reached on the inclusion of a clause mitigating the obligation to provide information. As a consequence, this obligation is now subject to 'taking into account the legitimate interests of operators'. In any case, the Working Group acknowledged that whereas the international framework should encourage the sharing of information, it remains up to the States to decide on the appropriate qualifiers regarding the shared information.

Lastly, the Working Group agreed to exclude space products from the scope of Building Block 14. This choice was made because establishing a system for the registration of space products would not have been in line with the principle of adaptive governance, given the presumably long time that will pass before space products materialize.

The final wording of Building Block 14 was agreed during the meeting of November 2019, by incorporation of minor, clarifying modifications to the previous draft.

15 Provision of Assistance in Case of Distress

1 Text

The international framework should provide for the applicability of Article V OST and the ARRA[(i)] to persons involved in space resource activities.

(i) 1968 Agreement on the Rescue of Astronauts, the Return of Astronauts and the Return of Objects Launched into Space.

2 Explanation

Building Block 15 deals with assistance in case of distress to persons involved in space resource activities, stipulating that a specific provision should be contemplated by the international framework in that regard. Inherent risks of space resource activities to persons on site or in the vicinity of space resource activities are thereby acknowledged, followed by reference to principles of related international *de lege lata* sources, *i.e.*, Article V OST and the ARRA.

As such, anyone participating or engaging in space resource activities, whenever operating on, near or in orbit of a celestial body, should be entitled to receive adequate and timely help by appropriate parties, in order to safeguard the health and well-being of any imperiled individuals. By contemplating a humanitarian perspective, Building Block 14 emphasizes the importance of cooperation and mutual assistance among all actors involved with those activities.

Distress is considered as a situation of peril where individuals are facing extraordinary, life-threatening conditions. Whenever exceptional circumstances of extreme urgency are endured, encompassing actual or imminent danger to persons involved with space resource activities, appropriate assistance should be envisaged and encouraged.

3 *Legal Basis*

Article V OST considers astronauts as 'envoys of mankind', entitled to assistance by States Parties in case of grave danger. As far as space resource activities are concerned, Article V OST specifically contemplates the situation of astronauts in outer space and on celestial bodies, which deserve 'all possible assistance', as follows:

> States Parties to the Treaty shall regard astronauts as envoys of mankind in outer space and shall render to them all possible assistance in the event of accident, distress, or emergency landing on the territory of another State Party or on the high seas. When astronauts make such a landing, they shall be safely and promptly returned to the State of registry of their space vehicle. In carrying on activities in outer space and on celestial bodies, the astronauts of one State Party shall render all possible assistance to the astronauts of other States Parties. States Parties to the Treaty shall immediately inform the other States Parties to the Treaty or the Secretary-General of the United Nations of any phenomena they discover in outer space, including the Moon and other celestial bodies, which could constitute a danger to the life or health of astronauts.

Whereas expressly mentioning assistance to astronauts in outer space and on celestial bodies, Article V OST codified, in general terms, paragraph 9 of the Declaration of Legal Principles, which states:

> States shall regard astronauts as envoys of mankind in outer space, and shall render to them all possible assistance in the event of accident, distress, or emergency landing on the territory of a foreign State or on the high seas. Astronauts who make such a landing shall be safely and promptly returned to the State of registry of their space vehicle.

Later, the ARRA expanded Article V OST, by regulating, more specifically in Articles 1 to 4, the humanitarian obligations of States Parties towards astronauts in the event of accident, distress or emergency landing. In the preamble, the treaty makes specific reference to '*sentiments of humanity*' leading the international efforts towards development of concrete expressions as far as the duty of assistance is concerned.

For the States Parties to the MA, its Article 10, paragraph 1 establishes that:

> States Parties shall adopt all practicable measures to safeguard the life and health of persons on the Moon. For this purpose they shall regard any person on the Moon as an astronaut within the meaning of article V of the Treaty on

> the Principles Governing the Activities of States in the Exploration and Use of Outer Space including the Moon and Other Celestial Bodies and as part of the personnel of a spacecraft within the meaning of the Agreement on the Rescue of Astronauts and the Return of Objects Launched into Outer Space.

Article 5, paragraph 2 MA further provides that:

> States Parties shall offer shelter in their stations, installations, vehicles and other facilities to persons in distress on the Moon.

4 *Alternatives Discussed*

The Building Block regarding assistance in case of distress was introduced for open discussion at the Working Group during its first face-to-face meeting in April 2016. Members and observers maintained a consistent position that no new rules were required on this topic because the principles of the OST and ARRA would be applicable. Since then, discussions revolved regarding the wording, in order to clarify that those principles should also apply to space resource activities. The final version of Building Block 14 was agreed in the face-to-face meeting of September 2016.

No alternative was contemplated in relation to the general terms of Building Block 14, and discussions centered solely on its exact wording. Thus, it reflected a rather non-contentious provision, since only specific and minor linguistic modifications were considered. Nevertheless, it was agreed that the issue of reimbursement of expenses for the rescue operations of astronauts involved with space resource activities is yet to be solved.

16 Liability in Case of Damage Resulting from Space Resource Activities

1 *Text*

16.1 The international framework should provide for the applicability of Articles VI and VII OST and the LIAB[(i)] to damage resulting from space resource activities.

16.2 The international framework should encourage initiatives of operators to provide, individually or collectively, compensation for damage resulting from their space resource activities.

(i) 1972 Convention on International Liability for Damage Caused by Space Objects.

2 *Explanation*

Liability resulting from space resource activities is addressed by Building Block 16 in two closely related paragraphs, which closely follow the applicable provisions of international space law.

Paragraph 16.1 states that, in case of damage, the international framework should promote reference to Articles VI and VII OST as well as to the LIAB. Whereas Article VI OST provides for the international responsibility of States Parties for their national space activities, irrespective of whether there are carried out by governmental or non-governmental entities, Article VII OST forms the link between a State's international responsibility and its international liability. The rules applicable to liability under the OST are further elaborated in LIAB, which develops the international regime related to damage caused by space objects.

Due to potential damage resulting from space resource activities, the international framework should properly acknowledge the referred provisions. By doing so, paragraph 16.1 establishes a clear link with *de lege lata* international instruments applicable, both in scope and effect, to space resource activities.

As a result of state responsibility and liability, States and international organizations are likely to address damage resulting from space resource activities in their national law and internal regulations. Compensation for damage resulting from space resource activities is considered in paragraph 16.2, which focuses specifically on operators. The provision encourages initiatives of operators to provide proper compensation, whether individually or collectively, and recommends addressing it in the international framework. An 'operator' is defined in Building Block 2, paragraph 2.6, as 'a governmental, international or non-governmental entity conducting space resource activities.'

3 *Legal Basis*

Building Block 16 explicitly indicates its legal basis by mentioning not only the treaties related to its subject matter but also, in the case of the OST, the specific norms concerned, *i.e.*, Articles VI and VII.

As already mentioned in the commentary to Building Block 5, Article VI OST addresses the international responsibility of States for national space activities, which includes those related to space resources:

> States Parties to the Treaty shall bear international responsibility for national activities in outer space, including the Moon and other celestial bodies, whether such activities are carried on by governmental agencies or by non-governmental entities, and for assuring that national activities are carried out in conformity with the provisions set forth in the present Treaty. The activities of non-governmental entities in outer space, including the Moon and other celestial bodies, shall require authorization and continuing supervision by the appropriate State Party to the Treaty. When activities are carried on in outer space, including the Moon and other celestial bodies, by an international organization, responsibility for compliance with this Treaty shall be borne both by the international organization and by the States Parties to the Treaty participating in such organization.

International liability emerging from damage caused by space activities in general is the subject of Article VII OST:

> Each State Party to the Treaty that launches or procures the launching of an object into outer space, including the Moon and other celestial bodies, and each State Party from whose territory or facility an object is launched, is internationally liable for damage to another State Party to the Treaty or to its natural or juridical persons by such object or its component parts on the Earth, in air space or in outer space, including the Moon and other celestial bodies.

Article VII OST reflects the Declaration of Legal Principles, in this case, of its paragraph 8:

> Each State which launches or procures the launching of an object into outer space, and each State from whose territory or facility an object is launched, is internationally liable for damage to a foreign State or to its natural or juridical persons by such object or its component parts on the Earth, in air space, or in outer space.

The principles regarding international liability for damage caused by space objects were further developed in the 1972 Convention which, in twenty-eight articles, introduced a special regime which also encompasses space resource activities. Building Block 16 does not define which provisions of the LIAB are to be considered, thus suggesting its full applicability.

For the States Parties to the MA, said treaty includes provisions concerning liability in Article 14, paragraph 2:

> States Parties recognize that detailed arrangements concerning liability for damage caused on the Moon, in addition to the provisions of the Treaty on Principles Governing the Activities of States in the Exploration and Use of Outer Space including the Moon and Other Celestial Bodies and the Convention on International Liability for Damage Caused by Space Objects, may become necessary as a result of more extensive activities on the Moon. Any such arrangements shall be elaborated in accordance with the procedure provided for in article 18 of this Agreement.

4 Alternatives Discussed

Liability in case of damage resulting from space resource activities was considered an important topic since the very beginning of the Building Blocks' drafting process. During deliberations, the risks related to these activities were accessed, as well as possible damage resulting therefrom. Related potentially hazardous activities were considered for comparison during the earlier sessions, such as terrestrial and deep-sea mining, as well as space activities involved with access to and use of space resources.

The original draft recognized that additional detailed arrangements may become necessary as a result of more extensive space resource activities, however this reference was removed after the face-to-face meeting in April 2016. Since September 2017, the wording of Building Block 16 has remained unchanged, indicating consensus in relation to its content and terminology.

17 Visits Relating to Space Resource Activities

1 Text

The international framework should provide for the applicability of Article XII OST, taking into account the legitimate interests of operators, including safety of operations and protection of intellectual property.

2 *Explanation*

Building Block 17 encourages transparency and confidence-building measures by indicating the relevance of visits relating to space resource activities while, at the same time, considering the legitimate interests of operators.

Installations and associated equipment devoted to space resource activities on celestial bodies are to be open for visitors, provided that reciprocity is ensued, and reasonable requirements are met. These prerequisites reflect justified concerns of operators, including safety of personnel, intellectual property rights and interference with normal operations. Therefore, authorization of visits *vis-à-vis* third parties should be granted by the operators on the basis of a request, provided applicable *sine qua non* conditions are observed.

Advance notice must be given of any projected visit, in order to ensure respect for operators' security and safety considerations, as far as space resource activities are concerned. Nevertheless, requests for visits should not be denied without reasonable cause, and require proper and timely justification.

Due to its subject matter, Building Block 17 should be considered in conjunction with Building Block 11, regarding technical standards for, and prior review of, safety zones around space activities.

3 *Legal Basis*

Article XII OST contains rules applicable to reciprocal visits to human-made structures on celestial bodies, as follows:

> All stations, installations, equipment and space vehicles on the Moon and other celestial bodies shall be open to representatives of other States Parties to the Treaty on a basis of reciprocity. Such representatives shall give reasonable advance notice of a projected visit, in order that appropriate consultations may be held and that maximum precautions may be taken to assure safety and to avoid interference with normal operations in the facility to be visited.

In the same sense, for the States Parties to the MA, paragraph 1 of its Article 15 contemplates, in relation to the Moon and other celestial bodies:

> Each State Party may assure itself that the activities of other States Parties in the exploration and use of the Moon are compatible with the provisions of this Agreement. To this end, all space vehicles, equipment, facilities, stations and installations on the Moon shall be open to other States Parties. Such States

Parties shall give reasonable advance notice of a projected visit, in order that appropriate consultations may be held and that maximum precautions may be taken to assure safety and to avoid interference with normal operations in the facility to be visited. In pursuance of this article, any State Party may act on its own behalf or with the full or partial assistance of any other State Party or through appropriate international procedures within the framework of the United Nations and in accordance with the Charter.

4 Alternatives Discussed

The topic was first considered as part of a single Building Block devoted to monitoring and inspection of space resource activities during the first face-to-face meeting of April 2016. At the time, a suggestion was made to develop a specific provision regarding visits, with reference to Article XII OST. During the following sessions an autonomous Building Block emerged, first named 'Inspection of space resource activities' and later, based on discussions developed during the face-to-face meeting of September 2017, titled as 'Visits relating to space resource activities.' At that opportunity, the final wording was agreed.

During early debates, when visitation was considered as part of a Building Block also devoted to monitoring and inspection, it was suggested to delete the Building Block devoted to the issue, because Article XII OST already covered it. At the time, it was also confirmed that, since visits to space resource activities would probably not occur in the near future, it would be unlikely for States to send manned missions to inspect foreign space resource activities, having to rely, for the time being, on remote sensing or small satellites, therefore different from the situation contemplated by Article XII OST.

At the last session of November 2019, the legitimate interests of the operators were clarified by inclusion of an additional reference, explaining that they include concerns related to safety of operations as well as protection of intellectual property rights.

18 Institutional Arrangements

1 Text

The international framework should provide for:

a. **The establishment and maintenance of a publicly available international registry for registering priority rights of an operator to search and/or recover space resources;**
b. **The establishment and maintenance of an international database, in addition to the international registry, for making publicly available:**

i. **Advance notifications of space resource activities, including any area-based safety measures;**
ii. **Information and best practices;**
iii. **The list of designated and internationally endorsed outer space natural and cultural heritage sites; and**
iv. **The list of designated and internationally endorsed sites of scientific interest;**
v. **Information and best practices on the prior authorization and continuing supervision of space resource activities for which States and international organizations are responsible;**
vi. **Notifications of the termination of space resource activities for which States and international organizations are responsible.**

c. **The designation or establishment of an international body or bodies responsible for:**
i. **The consideration and promotion of best practices;**
ii. **The listing of designated and internationally endorsed outer space natural and cultural heritage sites, and sites of scientific interest;**
iii. **The monitoring and review of the implementation of the international framework; and**
iv. **The governance of the international registry, the international database and any other mechanism that may be established for the implementation of the international framework.**

2 *Explanation*

Institutional arrangements are addressed in Building Block 18, which suggests the international framework to develop and create instances and bodies designed to facilitate the advancement of space resource activities. These international mechanisms are to be voluntarily opted-in by the relevant parties, at the proper time.

A publicly available international registry devoted to priority rights of an operator in relation to search and recovery of space resources would provide an efficient means of coordination, as indicated by subparagraph (a). Priority rights are addressed in Building Block 7 on access to space resources. Likewise, the obligation of States and international organizations involved in space resource activities to register those rights in accordance with the international framework is addressed in Building Block 14, subparagraph (a).

An open, public international database is suggested in subparagraph (b), designed to foster transparency and confidence-building by including the following information: (i) advance notification of space resource activities, also in relation to any area-based safety measures; (ii) information and best practices that may emerge; (iii) a catalogue of designated outer space natural and cultural heritage sites, as well as (iv) sites of scientific interest, duly endorsed internationally. Such sites are addressed in in subparagraphs (h) and (i) of Building Block 10 on avoidance and mitigation of potentially harmful impacts resulting from space resource activities.

Additionally, subparagraph (b) mentions information on (v) best practices on the prior authorization and continuous supervision of space resource activities, as well as (vi) notification of their termination, in relation to activities for which the applicable State or international organization is responsible.

The distinction between a register and a database, as indicated in Building Block 18, is important. While the former is composed of a formal or official systematic recording of items, the latter is a collection of data organized and arranged for easy search and retrieval. Therefore, subparagraphs (a) and (b) contemplate different arrangements, adapted to their particular objectives.

Finally, subparagraph (c) considers an international body or, eventually, bodies, to be designed or established in order to further strengthen the legitimacy and efficiency of the new international framework. Subparagraphs (i) to (iv) list the perceived responsibilities of this body: first, the consideration and promotion of best practices; second, a listing of designated and internationally endorsed, outer space natural and cultural heritages as well as sites of scientific interest; third, monitoring and review of the international framework; and fourth, the governance of the international mechanism developed for monitoring the implementation of the international framework.

Building Block 18 does not advocate, *per se*, the creation of an international organization devoted to space resource activities, nor does it exclude the possibility of this being eventually implemented by the relevant actors. Instead, the international registry, database and body (or bodies) considered are suggested as non-excluding alternatives to States and international organizations.

3 Legal Basis

The creation of an international registry is in line with Article I OST, which states:

> Outer space, including the Moon and other celestial bodies, shall be free for exploration and use by all States without discrimination of any kind, on a basis of equality and in accordance with international law, and there shall be free access to all areas of celestial bodies.

The provision on free access requires coordination at the international level in order to avoid interference with and between space resource activities. The international registry is also in line with the provision on promotion of international cooperation and understanding as enshrined in Article III OST:

> States Parties to the Treaty shall carry on activities in the exploration and use of outer space, including the Moon and other celestial bodies, in accordance with international law, including the Charter of the United Nations, in the interest of maintaining international peace and security and promoting international cooperation and understanding.

The establishment of an international database is in accordance with the information-sharing objective of Article XI OST:

> In order to promote international cooperation in the peaceful exploration and use of outer space, States Parties to the Treaty conducting activities in outer space, including the Moon and other celestial bodies, agree to inform the Secretary-General of the United Nations as well as the public and the international scientific community, to the greatest extent feasible and practicable, of the nature, conduct, locations and results of such activities. On receiving the said information, the Secretary-General of the United Nations should be prepared to disseminate it immediately and effectively.

For the States Parties to the MA, its Article 5, paragraph 1 provides that States are encouraged to submit information regarding their activities on the Moon to the Secretary-General:

> States Parties shall inform the Secretary-General of the United Nations as well as the public and the international scientific community, to the greatest extent feasible and practicable, of their activities concerned with the exploration and use of the Moon. Information on the time, purposes, locations, orbital parameters and duration shall be given in respect of each mission, including scientific results, shall be furnished upon completion of the mission. In case of a mission lasting more than sixty days, information on the conduct of the mission, including any scientific results, shall be given periodically, at thirty-day intervals. For missions lasting more than six months, only significant additions to such information need be reported thereafter.

4 Alternatives Discussed

The first face-to-face meeting in April 2016 considered the institutional arrangements needed for the establishment of the international legal framework. During the discussions, three institutions were suggested: (i) an international registry for the registration of exclusive rights of operators to search and recover space resources; (ii) an international repository of information; and (iii) an international fund for space resource activities, specifically dedicated to the interests of developing countries and for benefit-sharing.

As to the issue of having an international body for issuing licenses, it was suggested to strengthen coordination at the international level, but that States should continue to issue licenses and establish practices. The licensing framework could be inspired by either the IADC or ITU models, while the UNCLOS International Seabed Authority model was discarded.

The discussions on this issue were resumed at the face-to-face meeting of April 2017. The suggestion to establish three institutions (international registry, international repository and international fund) was maintained. In relation to the international registry, it was suggested that the UN should implement the registry, but no agreement was reached. Conversely, it was agreed that a specific provision on deorbiting, applicable for satellite operators, would be necessary. As to the international repository, it was discussed whether it would serve to identify the best practices and additional information on space resource activities, or whether it should only register priority rights. It was agreed that the implementation of such a body would be challenging and that it could be removed from this Building Block. Finally, as regards the international fund, the shift towards capacity building instead of only relying on monetary investment was discussed, and eventually it was suggested to remove the fund from the list and refer to it as an option in the context of benefit sharing in Building Block 13.

During the fourth meeting in September 2017, several changes were considered. In relation to the international registry, the final text stated that it would serve as a publicly available registry for priority rights of an operator to explore space resources. For the international repository, it was agreed that it would contain information and best practices, a list of designated natural or cultural heritage sites in outer space and a list of designated sites of scientific interest. The international fund was moved to Building Block 13. Finally, it was also suggested to address the creation of one or more additional international bodies responsible for the identification of best practices, listing space natural and cultural heritage sites, reviewing the implementation of the international framework and the governance of the international registry and international repository.

This Building Block was only re-examined during the meeting of April 2019, where the participants worked on the consolidated text and proposed new additions and commentaries. For the international registry, it was argued that it is not yet defined what information will be made publicly available. Additionally, it was decided to remove *in situ* from the final text, as it was already mentioned in Building Block 2. The international repository was renamed as 'international database', and it was suggested that it could be linked to the registry. Concerning both the registry and database, the members and observers agreed that the Building Block should not specify any procedures for preserving and maintaining natural and cultural heritage sites. It was also discussed that the Building Blocks did not specify whether the repository would only store and distribute information or whether it would be the sole body to identify best practices, although it is clear that the repository would be in charge of identifying best practices. Finally, a provision was included to the effect that information on advance notification on space activities, including area-based safety measures, would be made publicly available in the international repository.

19 Settlement of Disputes

1 *Text*

The international framework should encourage recourse by States, international organizations and operators to the resolution of disputes through adjudicatory, non-adjudicatory or hybrid mechanisms, for example by developing procedures for consultation or promoting the use of the 2011 Permanent Court of Arbitration Optional Rules for Arbitration of Disputes Relating to Outer Space Activities.

2 *Explanation*

By promoting the resolution of disputes involving space resource activities, Building Block 19 supports peaceful means for settlement of possible conflicts of interest involving States, international organizations and operators, in order to safeguard continuous, effective and sustainable space resource activities. As far as the current provision is concerned, the term 'disputes' should be understood as any disagreement between the parties involved.

Collaboration and cooperation between States, international organizations and operators are considered of fundamental importance for space resource activities. Nonetheless, disputes are expected to happen, due to the very nature of those activities. The recourse to peaceful means of dispute settlement is the cornerstone of the international legal framework for outer space.

Resolution of disputes is encouraged by Building Block 19 not only through adjudicative processes, which involves the determination of legal and factual issues by a neutral third party, through arbitration or judicial organs. Indeed, non-adjudicatory and hybrid mechanisms, involving non-judicial, consensual means such as conciliation, mediation and good offices are also considered.

Procedures for consultation are indicated as potential venues to prevent disputes, favoring a mutually satisfactory resolution for all parties involved. In general, those procedures involve direct negotiations between the parties in a cooperative and constructive spirit and carried out in good faith.

Building Block 19 does not categorize the many different methods available to the resolution of disputes, nor does it intend to promote a particular one in favor of others. But as an example, reference is made to procedures of consultation and the Permanent Court of Arbitration's Optional Rules for Arbitration of Disputes Relating to Outer Space Activities.[18] These rules are effective since December 6, 2011, and were developed based on the 2010 UNCITRAL Arbitration Rules, incorporating specific features applicable to outer space activities, including the public international element that pertains to potential disputes. These rules are flexible, privileging party autonomy and, as is the case in relation to the services of the Secretary-General and the International Bureau of the Permanent Court of Arbitration, are available to States, international organizations and private parties.

Resort to international mechanisms for peaceful solution of disputes does not, by itself, exclude the jurisdiction of domestic courts, available and applicable in accordance with the legislation of any given State, except as agreed between the parties and within the limits of international law.

3 *Legal Basis*

The peaceful resolution of disputes is embedded in many international instruments and institutions, working together or independently, encompassing different topics and a vast territorial scope.

In particular, Article 2, paragraph 3 of the Charter of the United Nations provides that 'all Members shall settle their international disputes by peaceful means in such a manner that international peace and security, and justice, are not endangered.' Additionally, Article 33 paragraph 1 of the Charter clarifies:

> The parties to any dispute, the continuance of which is likely to endanger the maintenance of international peace and security, shall, first of all, seek a solution by negotiation, enquiry, mediation, conciliation, arbitration, judicial settlement,

18 The Permanent Court of Arbitration is an international organization, with headquarters in The Hague, constituted by the Convention for the Pacific Settlement of International Disputes, 1899, to provide a forum for the resolution of international disputes through arbitration and other peaceful means.

> resort to regional agencies or arrangements, or other peaceful means of their own choice.

The OST does not present any specific dispute settlement mechanism for space activities, with the exception of the consultation mechanisms of Article IX and XII. Indeed, Article IX OST reads as follows:

> In the exploration and use of outer space, including the Moon and other celestial bodies, States Parties to the Treaty shall be guided by the principle of cooperation and mutual assistance and shall conduct all their activities in outer space, including the Moon and other celestial bodies, with due regard to the corresponding interests of all other States Parties to the Treaty. States Parties to the Treaty shall pursue studies of outer space, including the Moon and other celestial bodies, and conduct exploration of them so as to avoid their harmful contamination and also adverse changes in the environment of the Earth resulting from the introduction of extraterrestrial matter and, where necessary, shall adopt appropriate measures for this purpose. If a State Party to the Treaty has reason to believe that an activity or experiment planned by it or its nationals in outer space, including the Moon and other celestial bodies, would cause potentially harmful interference with activities of other States Parties in the peaceful exploration and use of outer space, including the Moon and other celestial bodies, it shall undertake appropriate international consultations before proceeding with any such activity or experiment. A State Party to the Treaty which has reason to believe that an activity or experiment planned by another State Party in outer space, including the Moon and other celestial bodies, would cause potentially harmful interference with activities in the peaceful exploration and use of outer space, including the Moon and other celestial bodies, may request consultation concerning the activity or experiment.

In turn, Article XII OST states:

> All stations, installations, equipment and space vehicles on the Moon and other celestial bodies shall be open to representatives of other States Parties to the Treaty on a basis of reciprocity. Such representatives shall give reasonable advance notice of a projected visit, in order that appropriate consultations may be held and that maximum precautions may be taken to assure safety and to avoid interference with normal operations in the facility to be visited.

Although consultation mechanisms are not regulated in depth by the OST, it is recognized that States shall be guided by the principle of cooperation and mutual assistance. Upon closer analysis of the wording, Article IX presents mandatory language, indicating that States 'shall' undertake appropriate international consultations, whereas Article XII uses the term 'may'.

These OST provisions are in line with the principle supported by paragraph 6 of the Declaration of Legal Principles:

> In the exploration and use of outer space, States shall be guided by the principle of cooperation and mutual assistance and shall conduct all their activities in outer space with due regard for the corresponding interests of other States. If a State has reason to believe that an outer space activity or experiment planned by it or its nationals would cause potentially harmful interference with activities of other States in the peaceful exploration and use of outer space, it shall undertake appropriate international consultations before proceeding with any such activity or experiment. A State which has reason to believe that an outer space activity or experiment planned by another State would cause potentially harmful interference with activities in the peaceful exploration and use of outer space may request consultation concerning the activity or experiment.

The LIAB presents procedures for both consultations at the diplomatic level and dispute settlement through the establishment of a Claims Commission. Article IX LIAB provides that a claim for compensation shall be presented via diplomatic channels or through the Secretary-General of the United Nations:

> A claim for compensation for damage shall be presented to a launching State through diplomatic channels. If a State does not maintain diplomatic relations with the launching State concerned, it may request another State to present its claim to that launching State or otherwise represent its interests under this Convention. It may also present its claim through the Secretary-General of the United Nations, provided the claimant State and the launching State are both Members of the United Nations.

According to Article XIV LIAB, whenever the diplomatic consultation procedure has failed to amicably settle the dispute, and one year after the initial notification, States may request the establishment of a Claims Commission:

> If no settlement of a claim is arrived at through diplomatic negotiations as provided for in article IX, within one year from the date on which the claimant

> State notifies the launching State that it has submitted the documentation of its claim, the parties concerned shall establish a Claims Commission at the request of either party.

The Claims Commission is empowered to make a final decision on the merits of the claim and to order compensation, if the parties so agree, pursuant to Articles XVIII and XIX LIAB:

> Article XVIII: The Claims Commission shall decide the merits of the claim for compensation and determine the amount of compensation payable, if any.
> Article XIX:
> 1. The Claims Commission shall act in accordance with the provisions of article XII.
> 2. The decision of the Commission shall be final and binding if the parties have so agreed; otherwise the Commission shall render a final and recommendatory award, which the parties shall consider in good faith. The Commission shall state the reasons for its decision or award.
> 3. The Commission shall give its decision or award as promptly as possible and no later than one year from the date of its establishment, unless an extension of this period is found necessary by the Commission.
> 4. The Commission shall make its decision or award public. It shall deliver a certified copy of its decision or award to each of the parties and to the Secretary-General of the United Nations.

For the States Parties to the MA, said treaty refers to inter-State consultations applicable in case a State has reason to believe that another State is not fulfilling its obligations under the Treaty or interferes with the rights of other States. Dispute settlement is also expressly referred to in Article 15, paragraph 3 MA, which however neither establishes nor recommends any specific dispute settlement mechanism.

Article 15, paragraph 3 MA provides as follows:

> If the consultations do not lead to a mutually acceptable settlement which has due regard for the rights and interests of all States Parties, the parties concerned shall take all measures to settle the dispute by other peaceful means of their choice appropriate to the circumstances and the nature of the dispute. If difficulties arise in connection with the opening of consultations or if consultations do not lead to a mutually acceptable settlement, any State Party may seek the assistance of the Secretary-General, without seeking the consent of any other State Party concerned, in order to resolve the controversy. A State

Party which does not maintain diplomatic relations with another State Party concerned shall participate in such consultations, at its choice, either itself or through another State Party or the Secretary-General as intermediary.

4 *Alternatives Discussed*

The Building Block on Settlement of Disputes was drafted during the first meeting in April 2016, in order to encourage the settlement of disputes between States, international organizations and operators. It was agreed that no supplementary body was needed and that the recourse to additional procedures, such as arbitration, required further discussion. Finally, the PCA ('Permanent Court of Arbitration') Rules were identified as a valuable option for the resolution of conflicts.

The discussion resumed during the meeting of April 2017. It was suggested that a better alternative could be to provide for State-to-State dispute resolution, excluding State-operator arbitration, and that a broad option for dispute settlement would be desirable.

In the meeting of September 2017, it was agreed that the international framework should encourage States, international organizations and operators to amicably settle their disputes. Although no specific dispute settlement mechanisms were mentioned, the Working Group did decide to include an express reference to the 2011 Permanent Court of Arbitration Optional Rules for Arbitration of Disputes Relating to Outer Space Activities.

Finally, it was agreed, at the November 2019 meeting, to remove the adjective 'amicable' to qualify the resolution of disputes, as it is unnecessary, and to add a clarification that recourse to adjudicatory, non-adjudicatory or hybrid mechanisms is encouraged.

20 MONITORING AND REVIEW

1 *Text*

Mechanisms should be developed for monitoring implementation of the international framework, for example on the basis of reports of States and international organizations, as well as for its review and further development consistent with the principle of adaptive governance.

2 *Explanation*

The development of mechanisms designed for monitoring the implementation of the international framework related to space resource activities is the topic of Building Block

20, which also takes into account future developments such as its review and further development.

Compliance is a concern of any international framework, and may be enhanced by the adoption of a wide range of monitoring mechanisms. Building Block 20 does not suggest any specific mechanism for this purpose, nor does it indicate its features. Instead, it emphasizes the importance of such instruments for space resource activities.

Irrespective of other available alternatives, Building Block 20 mentions the possibility of reports being prepared by States and international organizations, without going into detail regarding their periodicity or extent. Such reports are considered as relevant Transparency and Confidence Building Measures, by promoting transparency and limiting the possibility of disputes.

As in the Introduction and in Building Block 4, the term 'adaptive governance' is explicitly mentioned in Building Block 20.

3 *Legal Basis*

UN space treaties contain rules serving to the monitoring of their implementation: OST (Article XI) requires States Parties in a general manner to inform the Secretary General of the UN as well as the public and the scientific community of the nature and results of their space activities; this rule has been specified by the REG, especially by its Article IV requiring its State Parties to provide the UN Secretary General with the basic information concerning their space objects. The proposed provision is in line with this broadly accepted idea of reporting.

Concerning their amendment, all UN space treaties include respective provisions – OST in Article XV, ARRA in Article 8, LIAB in Article XXV, and REG in Article IX. The provision challenging the international mechanism to develop mechanism on its review and further development corresponds to these usual elements of international treaties.

4 *Alternatives Discussed*

Since introduced by the Working Group in its meeting of April 2016, Building Block 20 has maintained its structure and wording, indicating the non-contentious nature of this provision.

Appendix I

Consortium Partners, Members & Observers of the Working Group

Participants of the Working Group During the First Phase in 2016-2017

Members & Consortium Partners

Bargo	Cesar Perez	Catholic University of Santos	Brazil
Bittencourt Neto	Olavo	Catholic University of Santos	Brazil
Godden	Lee	CREEL, University of Melbourne	Australia
Latifulhayat	Atip	Indonesian Institute of Air and Space Law, Padjajaran University	Indonesia
Martinez	Peter	University of Cape Town	South Africa
Masson-Zwaan	Tanja	IIASL, Leiden University	The Netherlands
Simpson	Michael	Secure World Foundation	USA

Members

Acierno	Kyle	ispace	Japan
Al Rashedi	Naser	UAE Space Agency	UAE
Baseley-Walker	Ben	Planetary Resources	Luxembourg
Brisibe	Tare	National Space Research & Development Agency	Nigeria
Crawford	Ian	Birkbeck College	UK
Keravala	Jim	Off World, Inc.	USA
Kfir	Sagi	Deep Space Industries	USA
Khan	Imtiaz Ali	ISR	India
Link	Mathias	Ministry of the Economy	Luxembourg
Marchisio	Sergio	University La Sapienza	Italy
Mariez	Julien	CNES	France
Ramirez de Arellano	Rosa Maria	Mexican Space Agency	Mexico
Richards	Bob	Moon Express	USA
Sakamoto	Mitsuhiro	International Telecommunication Union	Switzerland
Sundahl	Mark	COMSTAC	USA

Wang	Guoyu	Institute of Space Law, Beijing Institute of Technology	China
de Wet	Sandea	Office of the Chief State Law Advisor	South Africa
Observers			
Abhijeet	Kumar	National Law School of India University	India
Antoni	Ntorina	Swiss Space Systems Holding	Switzerland
Arnould	Jacques	CNES	France
Barton	Matthew	EXPO 2020	UAE
Carpenter	James	ESTEC	The Netherlands
Castillo Olascoaga	Teresa	Mexican Space Agency	Mexico
Chan	Kimberly	Canadian Space Agency	Canada
Cheney	Thomas	University of Sunderland	UK
Christensen	Ian	Secure World Foundation	USA
Frank	Robin Jo	NASA	USA
Fujii	Kojiro	Nishimura & Asahi	Japan
Gabrynowicz	Joanne Irene	University of Mississippi	USA
Galache	J.L.	Aten Engineering	USA
Gold	Mike	COMSTAC	USA
Goncharova	Victoria	Embassy of Russia to the Netherlands	Russia
Hedman	Niklas	UNOOSA	Austria
Hobe	Stephan	Institute of Air and Space Law, Cologne University	Germany
Hofmann	Mahulena	University of Luxembourg	Luxembourg
Hunter-Scullion	Mitch	Asteroid Mining Corporation	UK
Ilves	Erika	Shackleton Energy Company	USA
Jah	Moriba	University of Arizona	USA
Kobata	Yuri	Ministry of Foreign Affairs	Japan
Kometani	Kazumochi	Ministry of Economy, Trade and Industry	Japan
Kozuka	Souichirou	Gakushuin University	Japan
Kunstadter	Chris	XL Catlin	USA
de Man	Philip	KU Leuven	Belgium
Marboe	Irmgard	University of Vienna	Austria
Marquez	Peter	Planetary Resources	USA
Martin	Anne-Sophie	University La Sapienza	Italy
Messina	Piero	ESA	France

Mijovic	Milan	SERBSPACE	Serbia
Muzyka	Kamil	Polish Space Exploration Group	Poland
Newman	Christopher	University of Sunderland	UK
Palkovitz	Neta	Innovative Solutions in Space B.V.	Netherlands
Di Pippo	Simonetta	UNOOSA	Austria
Rummel	John	McGill University	Canada
Smith	Lesley Jane	Leuphana University	Germany
Su	Jinyuan	Xi'an Jiaotong University	China
Tronchetti	Fabio	HowlyMo Law Firm, Beijing	China / USA
Tumlinson	Rick	Deep Space Industries	USA
Zeng	Siqi	Ministry of Foreign Affairs	China
Zhang	Zhenjun	China Institute of Space Law	China

Participants of the Working Group During the Second Phase in 2019-2020

Members & Consortium Partners

Bittencourt Neto	Olavo	Catholic University of Santos	Brazil
Christensen	Ian	Secure World Foundation	USA
Fujii	Kojiro	Nishimura Institute of Advanced Legal Studies	Japan
Hofmann	Mahulena	University of Luxembourg	Luxembourg
Ishido	Shimpei	Nishimura Institute of Advanced Legal Studies	
Latifulhayat	Atip	Indonesian Institute of Air and Space Law, Padjajaran University	Indonesia
Martinez	Peter	SpaceLab, University of Cape Town	South Africa
Masson-Zwaan	Tanja	IIASL, Leiden University	The Netherlands
Simpson	Michael	Ten To The Ninth Plus Foundation	Ireland

Members

Acierno	Kyle	ispace	Luxembourg
Al Rashedi	Naser	UAE Space Agency	UAE
Cheney	Thomas	Space Generation Advisory Council	UK
Crawford	Ian	Birbeck College	UK

Gold	Michael	MAXAR Technologies	USA
Hunter-Scullion	Mitch	Asteroid Mining Corporation	UK
Kfir	Sagi	Deep Space Industries	USA
Kriening	Torsten	PT Scientists	Germany
Link	Mathias	Ministry of the Economy	Luxembourg
Marchisio	Sergio	Agenzia Spaziale Italiana	Italy
Mariez	Julien	CNES	France
Nair	Praveen	ISRO	India
Porras	Daniel	UNIDIR	Mexico
Ramirez	Rosa Maria	Mexican Space Agency	Mexico
Reinohl	Michal	Ministry of Transport	Czech Republic
Rummel	John	COSPAR	USA
Sakamoto	Mitsuhiro	International Telecommunication Union	Japan
Sundahl	Mark	Cleveland-Marshall College of Law	USA
Supancana	Ida Bagus Rahmadi	Catholic University of Atma Jaya	Indonesia
Veneziano	Anna	UNIDROIT	Italy
Wang	Guoyu	Institute of Space Law, Beijing Institute of Technology	China
Welch	Chris	International Space University	France
De Wet	Sandea	Government of South Africa	South Africa
Yahaya	Isah Akor	National Space Research and Development Agency	Nigeria
Observers			
Abbud-Madrid	Angel	Colorado School of Mines	USA
Abhijeet	Kumar	National Law School of India University, Bangalore	India
Agnan	Marco	Odysseus Space	Israel
Aloia	Vinicius	Catholic University of Santos	Brazil
Alvarez	Tamara	New School for Social Research	UK
Arnould	Jacques	CNES	France
Baseley-Walker	Ben	Andart Global	USA
Black	Charles	Sen	UK
Blount	PJ	University of Luxembourg	Luxembourg
Burger	Edward	ESPI	Austria

Camacho	Sergio	National Institute of Astrophysics, Optics and Electronics	Mexico
Castillo Olascoaga	Teresa	Mexican Space Agency	Mexico
Checchia	Gabriele	Ambassador (ret.)	Italy
Clanton	Michael	Mothership Communications	USA
Cocco	Magda	Vieira de Almeida	Portugal
Correia Mendonca	Helena	Vieira de Almeida	Portugal
De Man	Philip	KU Leuven	Belgium
Dinsley	Ralph	Northern Space and Security Limited & Reflecting Space	UK
Di Pippo	Simonetta	UNOOSA	Austria
Eldholm	Maria	PT Scientists	Germany
Ellis	Kim	Earth and Space Technology Pty Ltd	Australia
Faires	Wes	Space Rights, LLC	USA
Ferreira	Luis	Airbus	Germany
Fuma	Kenji	Neural Inc.	Japan
Gabrynowicz	Joanne Irene	University of Mississippi	USA
Galache	JL	Aten Engineering, Inc.	USA
Gladysz	Blazej	Arendt & Medernach SA	Luxembourg
Goncharova	Victoria	Embassy of the Russian Federation in The Netherlands	Russia
Graps	Amara	Baltics in Space	Latvia
Hanlon	Michelle	For All Moonkind, Inc.	USA
Harrington	Andrea	Air Command and Staff College	USA
Hearsey	Chris	OSA Consulting	USA
Hedman	Niklas	United Nations Office for Outer Space Affairs	Austria
Hernandez	Sebastian	Trimble, Inc.	Spain
Hobe	Stephan	Institute of Air and Space Law, Cologne University	Germany
Huidobro	Marina	Catholic University of Santos	Brazil
Israel	Brian	Planetary Resources	USA
Jah	Moriba	The University of Texas at Austin	USA
Jeffreys	Rachel	UK Space Agency	UK
Johnson	Chris	Secure World Foundation	USA

Kaesmann	Oriane	Luxembourg Space Tech Angels Association	Luxembourg
Kapoglou	Angeliki	ESA	Netherlands
Keravala	Jim	OffWorld	USA
Keunen	Lisa	University of Glascow	UK
Khawar	Muhammad Abdullah	Engro Corp.	Pakistan
Khlystov	Nikolai	World Economic Forum	USA
Kozuka	Souichiro	Gakushuin University	Japan
Kumar	Saurabh	National Law University, Jodhpur	India
Kunstadter	Chris	XL Catlin	USA
Kyriakopoulos	George	National and Kapodistrian University of Athens	Greece
La Regina	Veronica	RHEA Group	Italy/The Netherlands
Lange	Ian	Colorado School of Mines	USA
Liang	He	Ministry of Foreign Affairs	China
Listner	Michael	Space Law & Policy Solutions	USA
Marboe	Irmgard	University of Vienna	Austria
Marinova	Aleksandra	Asteroid Mining Corporation	Bulgaria
Martin	Anne-Sophie	University La Sapienza	Italy
Masaki	Sugamiya	JAXA	Japan
Matuleviciute	Dovile	Ministry of the Economy	Luxembourg
Messina	Piero	ESA	France
Mijovic	Milan	SERBSPACE	Serbia
Miller	Zachary	VAERO Space Research, LLC	USA
Millwood	Scott	DLR Scientific Research Center (personal capacity)	Germany
Muzyka	Kamil	Polish Space Exploration Group	Poland
Neu	Juliette	Cingeto	USA
O'Brien	Dennis	The Space Treaty Project	USA
Ocasio-Christian	Jose	Caelus Partners	USA
O'Sullivan	Rhonda	Glencore	Australia
Othman	Mazlan	Academy of Sciences	Malaysia
Palkovitz	Neta	Innovative Solutions in Space B.V.	Netherlands

Profitiliotis	George	National Technical University of Athens	Greece
Ranyuk	Ekaterina	Roscosmos	Russia
Redchyts	Natalia	Ukrainian State Space Agency	Ukraine
Rhimbassen	Maria	University of Toulouse 1 Capitole	France/Canada
Rideout	Sally	Canadian Space Agency	Canada
Roberts	Ben	Moon Express	USA
Salmeri	Antonino	Asteroid Mining Corporation	Italy
Schingler	Jessy Kate	Open Lunar	USA
Shackleford	Scott James	Indiana University	USA
Simberg	Rand	Interglobal Media LLC	USA
Simpson	Carol	Ten to the Ninth Plus Foundation	USA
Smith	Lesley-Jane	Leuphana University	Germany
Spencer	Sam	Etiam Engineering	Australia
Stemmet	Andrea	Embassy of South Africa in The Netherlands	South Africa
Svec	Martin	Charles University	Czech Republic
Sweers	Jerre	Stellar Space Industries	Netherlands
Swiney	Gabriel	Department of State	USA
Takashi	Iwai	JAXA	Japan
Tronchetti	Fabio	HowlyMo - Beihang University	Italy/China
Tumlinson	Rick	New Worlds Institute	USA
Tung	Helen	Legal Futurist - Independent Consultant	Australia
Vannitsen	Jordan	Odysseus Space	Israel
Wang	Jilian	China Academy of Space Technology	China
Zhang	Zhenjun	China Institute of Space Law	China
Zhu	Juliette	Viant Commodities	China
Zoenen	Lynn	i-space	Luxembourg

Appendix II

Report of the Technical Panel

The Technical Panel was established in January 2018 in order to provide technical expertise regarding the content of the Building Blocks and to advise the Working Group on technical aspects of space resources governance issues. Kyle Acierno was the Chair of the Panel which was joined by Angel Abbud Madrid, Kieran Carroll, Matt Cosby, Lindy Elkins-Tanton, Mike Gold, Sebastian Hernandez, Deepika Jeyakodi, Jan King, Bob Lamboray, Hannah Lindberg, Attila Matas, Scott Millwood, Rhonda O'Sullivan, Maria Antonieta Perino, John Rummel, Mitsuhiro Sakamoto, Franz Schilling, Ben Schwarz, Alan Scott, Emilie Siemssen, Sam Spencer, Peter Stibrany, Chris Verhoeven, Maneesh Verma, Yuguang Yang and Lynn Zoenen. The Technical Panel reported to the Working Group during the meetings of April 2018 and November 2018 with its findings regarding improvements to the Building Blocks and suggestions for technical topics to be addressed in the framework of the governance of space resource activities.

The Technical Panel, in particular, chose to assess two critical topics in view of their urgency for industry/space agencies, to be progressed considering the several planned lunar missions. In view of the above, the panel divided its work into three teams, focusing on the critical issues respectively A. on the topics of frequency/orbit allocation for deep space missions, B. safety zones around space resource activities, and C. technical validation of the Building Blocks. The input of the Technical Panel was taken into account in the subsequent revisions of the Building Blocks and is indicated under the relevant sections of the Commentary. Some suggestions did not directly address the provisions of the Building Blocks or proposed topics for further research, outside the scope of the Working Group. Each team provided the Working Group with a report including recommendations, as provided below.

A Coordinating the Use of Radio Frequency and the Associated Orbit for Missions to and on Celestial Bodies ('Deep Space Missions')

The Team considered how the Building Blocks for the Development of an International Framework on Space Resource Activities interact with the international regulation on the coordination of the use of radio frequency and associated orbits for deep space missions and noted the following:

1 *Key Challenges*

The current position under ITU Regulations is that

- The ITU has a mandate to allocate and register radio frequencies for all radio services. For space services ITU registers radio frequencies, any associated orbital position in the geostationary satellite orbit and any associated characteristics of a satellite in other orbits including those relating to celestial bodies (e.g. Moon). Member States shall not assign to a station any frequency in derogation of the Table of Frequency Allocations in the Radio Regulations, which are Administrative Regulations of the ITU.
- Member States have practice of assigning lunar frequencies for 'research purposes', given absence of a commercial category and the fact that the current status of early commercial lunar ventures can also reasonably be classified as 'research'.'
- As commercial activities increase, the allocation of lunar radio frequencies should reflect the reality that a range of stakeholders are entitled to undertake on the Moon, including scientific research, lunar mission support, and commercial activities.
- At present, Member States are only able to assign lunar frequencies to radio stations around the Moon in the frequency bands allocated for 'research' purpose (space research service) or for operational purposes of spacecraft (space operation service).
- This requires the development of a framework for the ITU and/or the international community to effectively allocate lunar frequencies for commercial purposes as well.

2 *Objectives*

Given the strategic importance of the lunar environment and the prospect of a Lunar Gateway Project being established in the coming years, the team focused primarily on lunar orbits and frequencies in its consideration. What does the team want to achieve?

- To establish recommendations for a framework and process for access to lunar orbits and radio frequencies that appropriately balances the interests of a range of stakeholders, including national and international space organizations, commercial industry and scientific research;
- to establish an initial pathway from research allocations to commercial allocations, recognizing that a future framework should provide for the allocation of lunar orbits and radio frequencies for commercial purposes as well as scientific in order to provide certainty to all stakeholders;
- to establish a strategic Work Plan for 2019 with the specific goal of ensuring that this topic is raised as an agenda item by Member States at the next World Radio Conference (WRC) 2019;

- to recommend appropriate frequency bands and amount of spectrum for space missions to, and around, the Moon, including commercially-oriented missions.

3 *Strategic Recommendations*

The Technical Panel recommends

1. that getting this topic onto the Agenda of the next World Radio Conference (WRC) in 2019 or of a later date is treated as a strategic priority (noting that only Member States can propose agenda items);
2. that the Working Group prepares a high-level position paper which can be presented to Member States' Ministries/Departments on the issue, by the members of the Working Group, in order to receive support for the proposal of the topic as a WRC agenda item;
3. that the Working Group considers and aligns its position with that of other key stakeholders such as the Space Frequency Coordination Group (SFGG), Commercial SmallSat Spectrum Management Association (CSSMA), ITU, UNOOSA etc., ahead of the WRC 2019;
4. that further research is undertaken into the topics identified in this note, with the support of interns / researchers from organizations like ITU, UNOOSA, DLR and/or ESP;
5. that both synergies and possible areas of conflict between missions, scientific research and commercial activities' use of lunar frequencies are identified in order to accentuate the synergies and mitigate the risks of conflict.

4 *Recommendations for the Building Blocks*

Recommendation 1

We understand that the BB exclude non-physical resources, such as spectrum, from its definitions of 'Space Resource', 'Utilization of space resources' and 'Space Resource Activities.' However, as all Space Resource Activities will be undertaken primarily by automated/robotic technologies that require the support of radio communications, both with satellites in lunar orbit as well as terrestrial orbit and operational control rooms on both lunar and terrestrial surfaces. We recommend that the Working Group finds a way of acknowledging that frequencies are critical to all space activities, while remaining within the role it has established for itself.

Recommendation 2

The Building Blocks have adopted principles emphasizing the obligation to avoid the harmful interference between space activities, which is to be commended. However, perhaps the most likely interference between space activities is not a physical, but a technical one. Harmful interference between sophisticated lunar operations is most likely to occur through interference between frequencies. The risks to the safety of persons, the environment or property are in this way largely associated with technological interference which can be mitigated by an effective allocation of frequencies by the ITU.

Similarly, the response measures suggested in BB 11.2 might contemplate that the most likely responses will also be the technological ones, without undermining the ITU procedures established to deal with the interference between frequencies, which remain applicable to assignments related to the Moon.

Recommendation 3

A provision should be added to the Building Blocks requiring to 'notify frequency assignments for recording in the Master International Frequency Register in accordance with the Radio Regulations of the International Telecommunication Union.' This might clearly express the existing requirement to register orbits and frequencies for space resource activities.

Recommendation 4

The Building Blocks contemplates the protection of scientific sites in citing the aim of avoiding 'adverse changes to designated and internationally endorsed sites of scientific interest.' This emphasizes the need for protection of a physical site. However, the adoption of the concept of the 'integrity of scientific activities' might appropriately broaden the scope of what is to be protected. For example, under the Radio Regulations, the Shielded Zone of the Moon (SZM) where future Deep Space radars / telescopes will benefit from natural protection from terrestrial interference, is defined and protected. The narrow reference to 'scientific site' might therefore be replaced/or expanded, with a concept like the 'integrity of science' or 'the integrity of scientific activities.'

Recommendation 5

We recommend that the Working Group gives further consideration to the question of the 'damage' which will remain relevant under the OST and LIAB. In the telecommunications industry, damage to data through interference with systems and frequencies is often addressed through definitions of damage that include 'interference with the integrity of data.'

Further thought might be given to whether the BB wish to further develop the concept of damage related to interference in Space Resource Activities, which would not otherwise be captured by the narrower concept of one space object causing damage to another space object under OST and LIAB.

Recommendation 6

Outside of the Building Blocks, we recommend that the Working Group continues its positive engagement with the emerging space resource industry. This allows both New Space companies and traditional national space agencies to consider how their different needs can be met. We therefore recommend that the Working Group promotes discussion on the attached radio frequency bands for space research and space operation services that have been identified by the ITU (Attachment 1). This will assist future lunar stakeholders to identify their frequency requirements. These frequency bands are currently used for 'scientific or technical research purposes' for lunar activities in their development stage or for space operations. It appears that States are allocating these where applicable to commercial enterprise missions, because at this early stage such missions are similar to scientific missions.

However, as lunar activities increase and commercial objectives emerge, consideration will need to be given to how these frequencies are allocated to, for example, Lunar satellite services, Lunar mobile and broadband services etc. Seeking feedback from industry on whether the bands in Attachment 1 are both appropriate and/or sufficient, will help to shape our strategy for getting this issue onto the Agenda of the World Radio Conference 2023.

The Team had initially identified that New Space companies which are planning lunar and deep space missions will need access to three types of frequencies:

- S Band frequency for strong wireless connections between lander and rover.
- 900 MHz frequency for reliable wireless connections between lander and rover.
- X Band frequency for deep space telecommunications.

The S-Band and 900 MHz frequencies are used in a closed environment on the lunar surface with limited output power and do not interfere with other interplanetary frequencies. The range for X Band frequencies is set at 7 to 12 GHz and has several advantages for missions with small landers and rovers. These frequencies are efficient with small antennas and can handle higher power, while also providing a high bandwidth that supports imagery and HD Video. Historically, X Band Frequencies have been employed primarily by the NASA Deep Space Network. The most notable programs include the Voyager missions to Jupiter, the New Horizons mission to Pluto as well as the Curiosity rover on Mars.

There may also be new ways of communicating in the future, as developments in, for example, Quantum Technology make rapid advances. How such technology and frequencies might be utilized in the lunar environment and for future deep space missions should be further elaborated.

Recommendation 7

We have given very high-level consideration to the issue of 'paper satellites' that are sometimes used strategically to 'hold' slots in GEO. We recommend that the Working Group continues to be conscious that we should endeavor to learn from some of the practices and challenges of GEO allocation, to ensure that allocation of lunar frequencies and orbits are not used to exclude both commercial and scientific stakeholders from pursuing their lunar strategies. Such challenges are best addressed through the allocation model utilized by ITU. Further research will assist in developing ideas for future models further.

Recommendation 8

Finally, perhaps the most important question relating to the allocation of lunar radio frequencies and orbits is what model we should use for their allocation, to ensure that all States have access on the basis of equality and in accordance with international law. One question is whether we need a new ITU Frequency Allocation Table dedicated to lunar orbits and frequencies? And, whether the current framework for allocation of lunar and deep space frequencies will be adequate during an era of increased international participation by scientific, commercial and international stakeholders?

The ITU currently treats the allocation of frequency in GEO as a limited natural resource in which it uses a combined (1) first-come, first-served allocation and (2) reserved GEO slots for each Member State (See Art. 44 ITU Constitution). This model historically allowed more technologically advanced countries to pursue their national goals, while ensuring that other countries would not be denied access when they had sufficiently developed their space capacity in order to make use of GEO orbits. Whether such a model is also appropriate for lunar frequencies, is something that will no doubt generate much discussion amongst Member States.

United Nations Resolution 55/122 of 8 Dec 2000, which addresses the issue of access to non-planned frequency bands and services, notes that the first-come first-served mechanism may not lead to satisfactory outcomes for all countries, especially developing countries.[1] We have the opportunity to help shape the conversation now about how lunar frequencies and orbits should be allocated, through engagement amongst the Working Group, ITU, WRC-19 and 23, UNCOPUOS, and other fora.

Attachment 1 (Recommendation 6) – Lunar Frequencies

The following Regulations and Resolutions are relevant to lunar orbits and frequencies:

- Radio Reg. No. 1.23

1 *See* https://read.unilibrary.org/outer-space/international-space-law_2d91e4a3-en#page2.

- Radio Reg. No. 1.55
- Radio Reg. No. 1.111
- Radio Reg. No. 1.177
- Radio Reg. No. 4.24
- Radio Reg. No. 5.460
- Radio Reg. No. 22.22 relating to emissions in the shielded zone of the Moon
- Resolution 763 (WRC-15) Stations on Board Sub-orbital vehicles;
- UN res. 55/122 of 8 Dec 2000 which addresses the issue of access to non-planned frequency bands and services and notes that the first-come first-served mechanism may not lead to satisfactory results for all countries, esp. developing countries.[2]

The background on the allocation of lunar and deep space mission frequencies by ITU for 'scientific and technological research' follows below:

- Frequency bands are allocated to one or more terrestrial or space radio-communication services or the radio astronomy service in order to minimize and control interference.
- There are two key types of service relating to space radio-communications: first, satellite services and secondly, space research / space operation services.
- Frequency Allocations for satellite services (e.g. fixed-satellite service, mobile-satellite service, broadcasting-satellite service etc.) in use of satellite systems have been established considering interference scenarios involving artificial earth satellites (see No.1.111 of the Radio Regulation).
- Frequency bands allocated to satellite services cannot be used for radio-communication between Earth and a celestial body or on another celestial body because interference studies have not yet been conducted.
- As space resources are normally found on celestial bodies, the frequency bands allocated for satellite services will be difficult to be used for space resource activities, without a reform of the model of allocation.
- The frequency bands allocated for space research service (see Table 1) can be used for space resource activities as long as they are at the stage of scientific and technological research (See No.1.55).
- The frequency bands allocated to specifically space research service (deep space) can be used by radio-communication from or to spacecraft or other objects in deep space. The ITU defines deep space as Space at distances from the Earth equal to, or greater than, 2×10^6 km (see No. 1.177).
- Frequencies allocated for deep space can be used for near space communication under the condition specified in No.4.24 of the Radio Regulations. Although the frequency

2 *See* https://read.unilibrary.org/outer-space/international-space-law_2d91e4a3-en#page2.

band 7 190-7 235 MHz, allocated to space research, cannot be used by systems intended for deep space (see No. 5.460), all other frequency bands generally allocated to the space research service can be used for radio-communication from or to spacecraft or other objects in deep space. In addition, frequency bands allocated for space operation service can be used for space resource activities as long as their radio-communication is used exclusively for the operation of spacecraft.

- Special attention should be drawn to the No.22.22 of the Radio Regulations related to emissions in the shielded zone of the Moon.
- The frequency bands required for lunar and deep space commercial activities will not be sufficiently fulfilled by the frequency bands in Tables 1 and 2 (*i.e.* bandwidth required for space resource activities is beyond total bandwidth in Tables 1 and 2 taking into account the fact that the bands are already heavily used for the existing space research service and space operation services, or specific frequency band is necessary to conduct space resource activities from point of view of electromagnetic characteristics). Therefore, additional suitable frequency spectrum has to be identified.
- When space resource activities are further developed reaching a fully commercial stage (*i.e.* stage beyond activities for scientific and technological research purpose), the frequency bands allocated to space research will no longer be seen to be appropriate.
- A pathway for activities progressing from scientific research to commercial activities needs to be created, perhaps as a new service of allocated frequency bands for commercial space resource activities.
- It might also be useful to consider frequency allocation tables dedicated to communications within space in a certain area where no interference is foreseen from or to terrestrial radio-communications (*i.e.* radio-communications on the Earth) with appropriate conditions (direction of transmission and power).

Table 1 Allocation of frequency bands for space research

Frequency band	Table/ Footnote	Region	Categories and direction
30.005 - 30.01 MHz	Table	ALL	SPACE RESEARCH
137 - 138 MHz	Table	ALL	SPACE RESEARCH (space-to-Earth)
143.6 - 143.65 MHz	Table	ALL	SPACE RESEARCH (space-to-Earth)
400.15 - 401 MHz	Table	ALL	SPACE RESEARCH (space-to-Earth)
410 - 420 MHz	Table	ALL	SPACE RESEARCH (space-to-space)
1 215 - 1 300 MHz	Table	ALL	SPACE RESEARCH (active)
1 400 - 1 427 MHz	Table	ALL	SPACE RESEARCH (passive)
1 660.5 - 1 668.4 MHz	Table	ALL	SPACE RESEARCH (passive)

Frequency band	**Table/ Footnote**	**Region**	**Categories and direction**
2 025 - 2 110 MHz	Table	ALL	SPACE RESEARCH (Earth-to-space) (space-to-space)
2 110 - 2 120 MHz	Table	ALL	SPACE RESEARCH (deep space) (Earth-to-space)
2 200 - 2 290 MHz	Table	ALL	SPACE RESEARCH (space-to-Earth) (space-to-space)
2 290 - 2 300 MHz	Table	ALL	SPACE RESEARCH (deep space) (space-to-Earth)
2 690 - 2 700 MHz	Table	ALL	SPACE RESEARCH (passive)
5 250 - 5 255 MHz	Table	ALL	SPACE RESEARCH
5 255 - 5 570 MHz	Table	ALL	SPACE RESEARCH (active)
7 145 - 7 190 MHz	Table	ALL	SPACE RESEARCH (deep space) (Earth-to-space)
7 190 - 7 235 MHz	Table	ALL	SPACE RESEARCH (Earth-to-space)
8 400 - 8 500 MHz	Table	ALL (except SNG, CLN)	SPACE RESEARCH (space-to-Earth) (deep space 5.465)
8 550 - 8 650 MHz	Table	ALL	SPACE RESEARCH (active)
9 300 - 9 800 MHz	Table	ALL	SPACE RESEARCH (active)
10.6 - 10.7 GHz	Table	ALL	SPACE RESEARCH (passive)
13.25 - 13.4 GHz	Table	ALL	SPACE RESEARCH (active)
13.4 - 13.75 GHz	Table	ALL	SPACE RESEARCH
15.35 - 15.4 GHz	Table	ALL	SPACE RESEARCH (passive)
17.2 - 17.3 GHz	Table	ALL	SPACE RESEARCH (active)
18.6 - 18.8 GHz	Table	R2	SPACE RESEARCH (passive)
21.2 - 21.4 GHz	Table	ALL	SPACE RESEARCH (passive)
22.21 - 22.5 GHz	Table	ALL	SPACE RESEARCH (passive)
22.55 - 23.15 GHz	Table	ALL	SPACE RESEARCH (Earth-to-space)
23.6 - 24 GHz	Table	ALL	SPACE RESEARCH (passive)
25.5 - 27 GHz	Table	ALL	SPACE RESEARCH (space-to-Earth)
31.3 - 31.8 GHz	Table	ALL	SPACE RESEARCH (passive)
31.8 - 32.3 GHz	Table	ALL	SPACE RESEARCH (deep space) (space-to-Earth)
34.2 - 34.7 GHz	Table	ALL	• SPACE RESEARCH (deep space) • SPACE RESEARCH (Earth-to-space)
35.5 - 36 GHz	Table	ALL	SPACE RESEARCH (active)
36 - 37 GHz	Table	ALL	SPACE RESEARCH (passive)

Frequency band	Table/ Footnote	Region	Categories and direction
37 - 38 GHz	Table	ALL	SPACE RESEARCH (space-to-Earth)
40 - 40.5 GHz	Table	ALL	SPACE RESEARCH (Earth-to-space)
50.2 - 50.4 GHz	Table	ALL	SPACE RESEARCH (passive)
52.6 - 59.3 GHz	Table	ALL	SPACE RESEARCH (passive)
65 - 66 GHz	Table	ALL	SPACE RESEARCH
86 - 92 GHz	Table	ALL	SPACE RESEARCH (passive)
94 - 94.1 GHz	Table	ALL	SPACE RESEARCH (active)
100 - 102 GHz	Table	ALL	SPACE RESEARCH (passive)
105 - 122.25 GHz	Table	ALL	SPACE RESEARCH (passive)
148.5 - 151.5 GHz	Table	ALL	SPACE RESEARCH (passive)
164 - 167 GHz	Table	ALL	SPACE RESEARCH (passive)
174.8 - 191.8 GHz	Table	ALL	SPACE RESEARCH (passive)
200 - 209 GHz	Table	ALL	SPACE RESEARCH (passive)
217 - 231.5 GHz	Table	ALL	SPACE RESEARCH (passive)
235 - 238 GHz	Table	ALL	SPACE RESEARCH (passive)
250 - 252 GHz	Table	ALL	SPACE RESEARCH (passive)
2 501 - 2 502 kHz	Table	ALL	Space research
5 003 - 5 005 kHz	Table	ALL	Space research
10 003 - 10 005 kHz	Table	ALL	Space research
15 005 - 15 010 kHz	Table	ALL	Space research
18 052 - 18 068 kHz	Table	ALL	Space research
19 990 - 19 995 kHz	Table	ALL	Space research
25 005 - 25 010 kHz	Table	ALL	Space research
39.986 - 40.02 MHz	Table	ALL	Space research
40.98 - 41.015 MHz	Table	ALL	Space research
138 - 143.6 MHz	Table	R2,R3	Space research (space-to-Earth)
143.65 - 144 MHz	Table	R2,R3	Space research (space-to-Earth)
2 655 - 2 690 MHz	Table	ALL	Space research (passive)
3 100 - 3 300 MHz	Table	ALL	Space research (active)
4 990 - 5 000 MHz	Table	ALL	Space research (passive)
5 650 - 5 725 MHz	Table	ALL	Space research (deep space)
9 800 - 9 900 MHz	Table	ALL	Space research (active)
12.75 - 13.25 GHz	Table	ALL	• Space research (deep space) • Space research (space-to-Earth)

Frequency band	Table/ Footnote	Region	Categories and direction
13.75 - 14.3 GHz	Table	ALL	Space research
14.4 - 14.47 GHz	Table	ALL	Space research (space-to-Earth)
14.5 - 15.35 GHz	Table	ALL	Space research
16.6 - 17.1 GHz	Table	ALL	• Space research (deep space) • Space research (Earth-to-space)
18.6 - 18.8 GHz	Table	R1, R3	Space research (passive)
31 - 31.3 GHz	Table	ALL (except ARM, GEO, KZM, TJK, TKM)	Space research
34.7 - 35.2 GHz	Table	ALL (except ARM, AZE, BLR, RUS, GEO, KGZ, TJK, TKM)	Space research
74 - 84 GHz	Table	ALL	Space research (space-to-Earth)
138 - 143.6 MHz	5.210	CZE,G	Space research (space-to-Earth)
143.65 - 144 MHz	5.210	CZE,G	Space research (space-to-Earth)
174 - 184 MHz	5.233	CHN	SPACE RESEARCH (space-to-Earth)
258 - 261 GHz	5.256A	CHN, RUS, KAZ	SPACE RESEARCH (Earth-to-space)
400.15 - 401 MHz	5.263	ALL	SPACE RESEARCH (space-to-space)
449.75 - 450.25 MHz	5.286	ALL	SPACE RESEARCH (Earth-to-space)
470 - 485 MHz	5.291	R3	SPACE RESEARCH (space-to-Earth)
1 370 - 1 400 MHz	5.339	ALL	Space research (active)
2 640 - 2 655 MHz	5.339	ALL	Space research (active)
4 950 - 4 900 MHz	5.339	ALL	Space research (active)
1 700 - 1 710 MHz	5.384	IND, INS, J	SPACE RESEARCH (space-to-Earth)
1 750 - 1 850 MHz	5.386	R2 (except MEX), AUS, GUM, IND, INS, J	SPACE RESEARCH (Earth-to-space)
4 200 - 4 400 MHz	5.437	ALL	Space research (passive)
5 650 - 5 725 MHz	5.454	AZE, RUS, GEO, KGZ, TJK, TKM	SPACE RESEARCH (deep space)
8 400 - 8 500 MHz	5.466	SNG, CLN	SPACE RESEARCH (deep space 5.465)
14.5 - 14.8 GHz	5.509G	ALL	SPACE RESEARCH (Earth-to-space)
25.5 - 27.5 GHz	5.536	ALL	INTER-SATELLITE(SPACE RESAECH (space-to-space))

Frequency band	Table/ Footnote	Region	Categories and direction
31 - 31.3 GHz	5.545	ALL (except ARM, GEO, KZM, TJK, TKM)	SPACE RESEARCH
34.7 - 35.2 GHz	5.550	ARM, AZE, BLR, RUS, GEO, KGZ, TJK, TKM	SPACE RESEARCH
78 - 79 GHz	5.560	ALL	Radars located on space station in SPACE RESEARCH

Table 2 Allocation for space operation service

Frequency band	Table/ Footnote	Region	Categories and direction
30.005 - 30.01 MHz	Table	ALL	SPACE OPERATION (satellite identification)
137 - 138 MHz	Table	ALL	SPACE OPERATION (space-to-Earth)
272 - 273 MHz	Table	ALL	SPACE OPERATION (space-to-Earth)
401 - 402 MHz	Table	ALL	SPACE OPERATION (space-to-Earth)
1 427 - 1 429 MHz	Table	ALL	SPACE OPERATION (Earth-to-space)
1 525 - 1 535 MHz	Table	ALL	SPACE OPERATION (space-to-Earth)
2 025 - 2 110 MHz	Table	ALL	SPACE OPERATION (Earth-to-space) (space-to-space)
2 200 - 2 290 MHz	Table	ALL	SPACE OPERATION (space-to-Earth) (space-to-space)
267 - 272 MHz	Table	ALL	SPACE OPERATION (space-to-Earth)
400.15 - 401 MHz	Table	ALL	SPACE OPERATION (space-to-Earth)
148 - 149.9 MHz	5.218	ALL	SPACE OPERATION (Earth-to-space)
163 - 167 MHz	5.230	CHN	SPACE OPERATION (space-to-Earth)
174 - 184 MHz	5.233	CHN	SPACE OPERATION (space-to-Earth)
258 - 261 GHz	5.256A	CHN, RUS, KAZ	SPACE OPERATION (Earth-to-space)
433.75 - 434.25 MHz	5.281	R2, IND	SPACE OPERATION (Earth-to-space)
433.75 - 434.25 MHz	5.281	F, B	SPACE OPERATION (Earth-to-space)
449.75 - 450.25 MHz	5.286	ALL	SPACE OPERATION (Earth-to-space)
470 - 485 MHz	5.291	R3	SPACE OPERATION (space-to-Earth)
549.75 - 550.25 MHz	5.298	IND	SPACE OPERATION (space-to-Earth)
1 750 - 1 850 MHz	5.386	R2 (except MEX), AUS,	SPACE OPERATION (Earth-to-space)

Frequency band	Table/ Footnote	Region	Categories and direction
		GUM, IND, INS, J	
7 100 - 7 155 MHz	5.459	RUS	SPACE OPERATION (Earth-to-space)
7 190 - 7 235 MHz	5.459	RUS	SPACE OPERATION (Earth-to-space)

B Establishing, Maintaining and Terminating Safety Zones for the Extraction of Extraterrestrial Resources

The Team tackled the issue of establishing safety zones on the Moon, asteroids, or other celestial bodies. Its main directions were the following:

- There is an increasing need to coordinate safety zones in order to control the traffic from different upcoming missions and to avoid harmful interference with other missions, including potential impacts on designated lunar heritage sites.
- Currently there is a lack of clarity of the technical requirements that companies need to successfully implement to protect their mission and to guarantee the safety in the proximity of others, as well as the protection of the environment.
- The methodology for determining safety zones inherently varies widely depending upon the celestial body where an operation is taking place and the nature of the activity. Therefore, the Team found that it would be impossible to establish a single means of deciding how safety zones should be determined. Instead, following the example of the Outer Space Treaty, the Team developed a series of Guiding Principles that can be universally adopted and implemented in a manner which addresses the unique circumstances of each environment and activity.

1 Key Challenges

The key challenge for the Team was to adopt a procedure that companies and countries can leverage to determine a safety zone regardless of the environment or activities. Again, the Team decided that the best means of accomplishing this goal was to adopt a series of Guiding Principles that can be followed to support safe operations in compliance with Article IX of the Outer Space Treaty.

2 *Guiding Principles*

Principles for Establishing, Maintaining, and Terminating Safety Zones for the Extraction of Extraterrestrial Resources

The following principles have been developed by the Team to govern establishing and maintaining safety zones for the extraction of extraterrestrial resources on the Moon, asteroids, or any other celestial body:

i. Safety zones should be established, maintained, and terminated in a manner that protects public and private personnel, equipment, and operations from harmful interference.
ii. Safety zones will be established, maintained, and terminated in a manner that fully complies with the Treaty on Principles Governing the Activities of States in the Exploration and Use of Outer Space, including the Moon and Other Celestial Bodies.
iii. Safety zones should be established by determining the area in which nominal operations of the relevant activity or an anomalous event could reasonably cause harmful interference with other parties' personnel, equipment, or operations.
    a. The size and scope of a safety zone will take into account the environment of the relevant celestial body and the nature of the operations being conducted.
    b. The size and scope of the safety zone will be made in a reasonable manner leveraging commonly accepted scientific and engineering principles.
    c. If the nature of the operation on a celestial body changes, the size and scope of a safety zone will be altered accordingly and may be terminated when the operation ceases.
iv. The entity establishing, maintaining, or terminating a safety zone shall be able to publicly provide the applicable basis for the zone to the extent practicable without violating national export control laws or the confidentiality of commercial information and/or intellectual property.
v. Safety zones shall be applied in a manner that encourages the robust, safe, and efficient extraction and utilization of space resources.

3 *Example*

The following example illustrates how the principles described above could be implemented.

Company A has resource extraction equipment on the Moon and seeks to establish a safety zone in order to protect its own operations, as well as any other actors and operations that are on the Moon while Company A's activities are taking place. The equipment is registered on Country A's registry of space objects. The equipment is not scheduled to move for another five years, when Company A will send a vehicle capable of moving the equipment to another location on the Moon. Company A conducted tests on the equipment in a simulated lunar environment laboratory on Earth. Those tests showed that during normal operations, the equipment kicks lunar regolith up to 10 meters from the location of the equipment. The tests also showed that during the most disastrous anomalous event possible (*i.e.* an explosion), the resulting debris landed up to 15 km from the location of the equipment. Company A sent basic information regarding the nature of the tests that were conducted to the United Nations Secretary General and the Director of the United Nations Office for Outer Space Affairs (UNOOSA) in support of establishing a safety zone of 20 km. Company A also published similar information on its website to ensure broad public awareness. Five years later, Company A conducts similar tests based on a new location to which it will move its extraction equipment. Company A again sends the results of those tests to the UN Secretary General and publishes the information on its website, along with a declaration of a modified safety zone, based on the new test results.

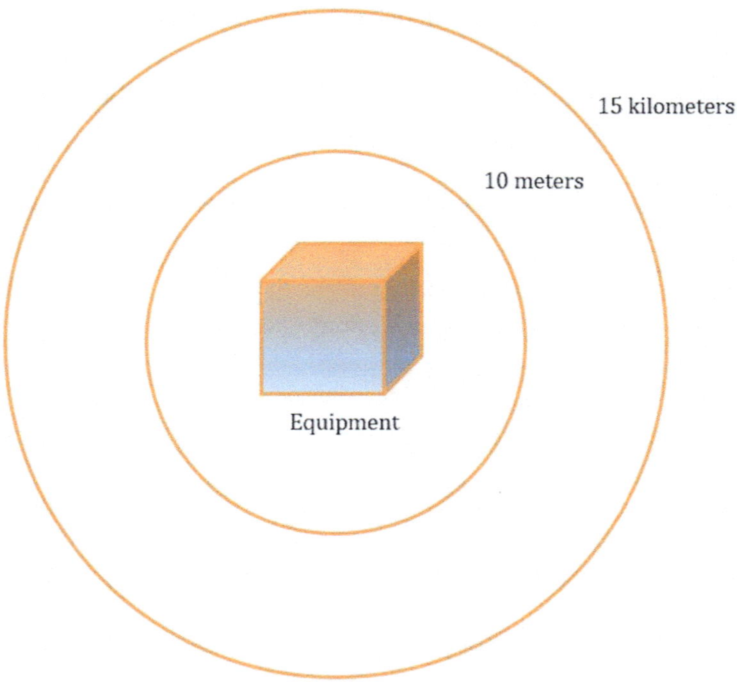

1. Company A's actions are in accordance with Principle I because it is seeking to establish a safety zone that helps to keep other actors, operations, and equipment on the Moon safe from harm.
2. Company A's actions are in accordance with Principle II because they comply with the principles of the Outer Space Treaty.
3. Company A's safety zone is in accordance with Principle III because it was established by leveraging commonly accepted scientific and engineering principles that were utilized in the simulated lunar environment laboratory to account for the unique environment of the relevant celestial body (with a distance added to provide for the potential margin of error), and was altered to account for a subsequent change in the nature of the operation.
4. In accordance with Principle IV, Company A shared the information regarding its testing and subsequent results with the United Nations and the general public via its website. The information provided was basic and therefore did not violate national export control regulations or any proprietary business restrictions.
5. Company A's safety zone was utilized in accordance with Principle V because it allowed for robust resource extraction activities during the five-year period, ensured the safety of Company A's operations while protecting other actors on the Moon, and provided for the efficient use of the area by updating the safety zone's status when changes to the activity occurred.

4 *Strategic Recommendations*

Team 2 makes the following recommendation to The Hague International Space Resources Governance Working Group (the 'Hague Working Group'):

At the upcoming Legal Subcommittee meeting of the Committee on the Peaceful Uses of Outer Space, The Hague International Space Resources Governance Working Group members should request that their national delegations explicitly express their support for the Guiding Principles.

C Key Observations and Recommendations

The Team worked towards providing recommendations with regard to the Building Blocks and the technical aspects of space resource activities. Among the elements that were highly welcome by the Team the adaptive governance approach played a central role; according to the majority of its members, this governance method is the underlying pillar of the future of space resources utilization. Furthermore, the Team 3 notes that the suggested benefit sharing mechanism is a major milestone in space resource utilization law as no other framework has ever specified any implementation measures. Another very well received aspect of the Building Blocks is the fact that the needs of industry stakeholders have been mostly taken into account.

1 *Key Recommendations*

i. Clarify the provisions of the principle of the 'benefit for and in the interest of all countries and humankind':
   - In the body of the Building Blocks, the phrase 'the needs of developing and emerging countries shall be taken into account particularly' should be replaced by the wording 'shall ensure a level-playing field between all countries', in order to treat all countries equally.
   - The condition of respecting the 'interests of all countries and humankind' (*i.e.* no harm on Earth, basic conditions, etc.) should be specified and enlarged by a provision making a clear distinction between the interests and the benefits. In the same vein, benefit-sharing 'irrespective of economic and scientific development' of the countries should be guaranteed through the promotion of the participation by all countries in space resource activities.
   - The phrase 'exchange of expertise and technology among States on a mutually acceptable basis' should be replaced by an 'exchange of expertise and technology among States upon common agreement.'

ii. The implementation of adaptive governance
   - A periodic review for the regulation of space resource activities should be introduced in order to ensure an innovation-friendly climate at all times (avoiding a similar situation as we have it today – outdated laws due to lack of progress in legislation on the utilization of space resources over the past 50 years). The Team suggests thinking on similarly flexible models like the ITU that has adopted a 4-year review.
   - The body or organization be responsible for the review should be specified.

iii. Eliminate contradictions regarding the 'access to space resources'
   - While the text introduces the attribution of priority rights to an operator to search for space resources, it also allows for unrestricted search for these resources. This might imply problems of overlapping (Example: if a resource can be extracted by entity A, entity B shall not be able anymore to have unrestricted search within that area).
   - The phrase 'the international framework should enable the unrestricted search for space resources' should be replaced by 'the international framework should enable the unrestricted remote sensing for space resources.'

iv. Clarify the rights and obligations of private sector participants

- The future international framework should not address only States and intergovernmental organizations but also private companies and individuals.
- The principle embodied in the original version of the Building Blocks stating that 'operators should be encouraged to provide for benefit-sharing' should be clarified. In how far shall States directly request something from operators? How free are countries in implementing the international framework or find solutions without consulting operators?
- Private sector participants and governments should be involved in the designation or establishment of an international body responsible for the identification of best practices of the utilization of space resources.
- The international framework should provide legal certainty not only for 'operators' but also for the 'owners' of private companies dealing with space resources activities, including their shareholders.
- The results of space resource activities shall enter the international repository on information and best practices 'to the greatest extent feasible and practicable for operators' in order to keep administrative paperwork at a low level.
- Article XII OST states that 'all stations, installations, equipment and space vehicles on the Moon and other celestial bodies shall be open to representatives of other States Parties to the Treaty on a basis of reciprocity.' The Building Blocks mention that the international framework should take into account the 'legitimate interests of operators.' These should be specified granting them full autonomy and control over stations, installations, equipment and space vehicles.

v. Clarify key responsibilities
  - It should be clarified who will be responsible for the conduct of a review/risk assessment prior to the authorization of a space resource activity in order to ascertain that such an activity is carried out in a safe manner avoiding harmful impacts.
  - The responsibilities for the development of a methodology to assess that equipment, operational procedures and processes applied in space resource activities meet common technical standards should be defined. The industry should be given an opportunity to provide input and clarify what's meant by 'common technical standards.'
  - On the technical standards for equipment, the standardization should be reflected and developed on the basis of existing examples (ASTM, ANSI, ASME, BSI, ISO, NFPA, AS, etc.).
  - It should be specified which intergovernmental technical office/organization/entity would be responsible for monitoring and implementing containment/countermeasures in case of harmful impact given that this task implies an important commitment (investigations, regular technical reports and periodical checks).

- Investigations and technical reports on adjusted and terminated activities shall be established and shared in a transparent way by the responsible intergovernmental organization/office.
- In case of a harmful impact, States/intergovernmental organizations which authorized the space resource activity shall not only implement measures to respond to these, but also apply containment and countermeasures to redress such harmful impact: Such respond does not necessarily imply any concrete action concerning the damage that was caused by the activity,

vi. Clarify the ownership of the material
- In the context of a notification of the termination of space resource activities, including the statement on the condition of the area where the space resource activity was carried out, it remains to be clarified whether the material left behind will continue to be owned by the company that has carried out the space resource activity or whether it will become common property: *i.e.* what will happen to company XY's rover after the relative mission is finished?
- Priority rights for processing of space resources (in addition to searching and recovering), not only *in situ*, but also for bringing them back to Earth should be provided.

vii. Clarify wording and definitions
- The definition of 'safe utilization' of space resources should be enlarged by the condition that their orderly and safe utilization shall 'respect the terrestrial and extraterrestrial environment and humankind.'
- The difference between Space Object and Space Products should be clarified:
  - Do the Space Products need to be sold to qualify as a product and do they have to be registered? An introduction of examples of such products should be deliberated: 'Space Products may include, but should not be limited to, propellants, refined metals, plastics, refined gases (e.g. H2, O2, CO2), etc.).'
  - Do Space Products and/or Space Objects include debris? If so, the qualification 'including after the end of operating life, until the final destruction or re-use in another operating Earth-based or Space-based Space Object' should be added to the definition(s).

Appendix III

Report of the Socio-Economic Panel

The Socio-Economic Panel was established in June 2018 with the purpose to function as research and analysis arm to complement the functions of the Working Group, particularly in identifying the socio-economic challenges of space resource utilization and advising the Working Group about current developments and the feasibility of the implementation of the Building Blocks. In particular, the Socio-Economic Panel provided input on the socio-economic aspects associated with the Building Blocks, including the sharing of benefits related to space resources utilization, the financing aspects and environmental impact of space resource activities, as well as the historical significance of space resources.

The interdisciplinary panel was chaired by Ian Christensen and consisted of Marcia Alvarenga, Tamara Alvarez, Sergio Camacho, Gabriele Checcia, Kenji Fuma, Thema Iso, Muhammad Abdullah Khawar, Nikolai Khlystov, Ian Lange, Dovilė Matuleviciute, Juliette Neu, George Profitiliotis, and Giuseppe Reibaldi. The Socio-Economic Panel reported to the Working Group during the meetings of November 2018 and April 2019 and produced four whitepapers on the following topics:

1. capacity building for benefiting from the exploration and utilization of space resources,
2. international cooperation models,
3. principles of responsible investment for space resources, and
4. social license to operate.

Some of the recommendations of the Socio-Economic Panel were implemented in the discussion and revision of the Building Blocks, and are included under the relevant provisions of the Commentary. The rest of the Panel remarks initiated further discussion, but addressed topics that are not included in the Building Blocks. Hereafter are the main results for each white paper.

A Recommendations on Capacity Building Programs for Benefiting from the Exploration and Utilization of Space Resources

1 Introduction

Building Block 13 calls for sharing of benefits arising out of the utilization of space resources – with an emphasis on non-monetary benefits. A fundamental assumption that is made in many of suggested benefit types is increased participation in aspects of space resource activities from actors in states that are not among the leading spacefaring nations. In this whitepaper the Socio-Economic Panel provides commentary for consideration for the development of space resources related capacity building programs as an element of the implementation strategy for Building Block 13.

In line with Building Block 13 for the Development of an International Framework on Space Resource Activities, States and intergovernmental organizations authorizing and supervising space resource activities shall provide for benefit-sharing by promoting the participation in space resource activities by all countries, in particular developing countries, irrespective of their economic and scientific development. Recognizing that countries have very different space capacities and in order to create an enabling environment for participating in and benefiting from space resource activities, the international framework should provide for capacity development programs for all interested countries, in particular developing countries.

Investment in space science and technology is perceived by many policy-makers in developing countries as a waste of financial resources that could be used to solve problems that the country has. The fact is, new exploration of space resources and innovative applications of the acquired scientific and technological knowledge will translate into socioeconomic benefits not only in space but also on Earth. The awareness of benefits on Earth that can be derived from participating in space resource activities would broaden the base of policy- and decision-makers in developing countries interested in using advanced technologies in national development programs.

Traditionally, the development of science has been an area for international cooperation. Activities that include space-emerging and other developing countries in advancing the science and technology of space resources should be strengthened. Efforts should be made to invite more non-spacefaring countries to join existing and future international space exploration programs. Capacities built in this manner will expedite the development of an International Framework on Space Resource Activities.

The United Nations Committee on the Peaceful Uses of Outer Space (UNCOPUOS), whose activities are effectively supported by the United Nations Office for Outer Space Affairs (UNOOSA), is a unique international forum for decision-making, guidance, coordination, information-sharing and opening up collaboration on a global scale in all space-related matters and in particular, in space exploration. Through one of its initiatives, UNCOPUOS tries to ensure that all countries, both industrialized and developing, at the governmental level and at the non-governmental level (*i.e.* industry, the private sector, civil society and younger generations), can participate in and benefit from space exploration and innovation.

The exploration and utilization of space resources will likely involve lengthy discussion on the meaning of terms to be contained in the evolving text of the Building Blocks of the proposed international framework. Agreeing on the terminology will include reaching a common understanding, among others, of what is meant by space resources, space activities, celestial bodies, space exploration, extraction and exploitation of space resources. To participate in the development of the international framework or just to understand the 'rules of the game' to participate in space resource activities will require capacity building on existing international space law and accepted non-binding guidelines and practices. This capacity building will be required for industrialized and developing countries to understand the scope and principles of the international framework proposed, including access and utilization of space resources

2 *Review of Existing Status of Capacity Building Programs Related to Space Resources*

Members of the Socio-Economic Panel undertook a review of existing capacity building programs in the space sectors in order to ascertain any existing activities specifically related to capacity building. This review resulted in three primary findings:

Finding 1: No existing international program/center focused specifically on capacity building for space resources development or utilization
In the space community capacity building programs are common, but typically focus on capacity to use and benefit from satellite applications (e.g. remote sensing, disaster response, telecommunications, etc.) or on expanding space science capabilities. Capacity building programs are particular common in the Earth observation community, for one example see the Working Group on Capacity Building and Data Democracy (WGCapD) under the Committee on Earth Observation Satellites (CEOS). In the case of the WGCapD, agencies are invited to nominate representatives to plan and implement approved capacity building activities. In turn, the experiences, best practices, lessons learned and capacity building resources of participating agencies (*i.e.* members of WGCapD) are used to develop training activities for each year.

The WGCapD undertakes a variety of activities based on the four pillars of the Data Democracy Initiative Mission and aims to unify CEOS efforts toward:

- Providing wider and easier access to Earth Observation data.
- Increasing the sharing of software tools such as the use of open source software and open systems interface.
- Increasing data dissemination capabilities and transferring relevant technologies to end users.

- Providing intensive capacity building, education, and training (including awareness and outreach) for enabling end users to gather the information they need and for increasing communication on achieved results.
- Developing case models for articulating and measuring the benefits that might arise.

While no existing large-scale space resources focused capacity building program exists – the take away is that capacity building in the EO community is very dynamic and evolving rapidly. The space resources sector might follow some of the existing capacity building models and possibly even use some of the available open source resources to achieve its objectives.

Finding 2: Regional Centers for Space Science and Technology Education affiliated to the United Nations do not currently address space resources specifically
UNOOSA-affiliated Regional Centers for Space Science and Technology Education exist in Africa (Nigeria and Morocco), Latin America (Mexico and Brazil), India, Jordan, and China. These Centers currently have curricula focused on:
- Satellite Metrology;
- Satellite Communications;
- Space and Atmospheric Science (addresses some topics related to space resources);
- Remote Sensing and Geographic Information Systems (addresses some topics complementary to space resources);
- Global Navigation Satellite System; and
- Space Law.

There is currently no curriculum focused specifically on space resources. A further gap relates to outreach and space literacy. These curricula and Regional Centers were developed a set of comprehensive capacity building activities targeted to a space-interested stakeholder group. It was assumed that those participants had some exposure to space subjects. In order to truly reach out to all potentially interested participants in space resource activities, the community will need to think about implementation that involves basic access and outreach to stakeholder who may have no prior involvement in space-related activities.

Beyond the UNOOSA-Affiliated Regional Centers, there are a number of communities working on working on space exploration and innovation, in a context that includes emerging space nations. The scope of space exploration goes well beyond the science and technology involved in space resource activities. Nevertheless, much of the knowledge needed for space resource activities is being developed by national and international, working groups and forums working on inter-planetary missions, space weather, space debris, near-Earth objects, particularly asteroids, and space situational awareness. Non-governmental organizations such as the International Astronautical Federation, the

International Academy of Astronautics, the International Institute of Space Law and the International Law Association, as well as international forums such as the Committee on Space Research, the International Mars Exploration Working Group, the International Lunar Exploration Working Group, the International Space Exploration Coordination Group and the International Space Exploration Forum, support collaboration, exchange of information, data and coordination.

Countries with emerging or limited capabilities in space exploration can be included in various space activities. Initially, this may involve the dissemination of information as well as targeted capacity building. Small ground-based facilities, such as those for space environment monitoring and astronomical observation of asteroids and access to data archives, may act as a gateway to the development of national capabilities in space science.

Finding 3: A small number of domestic & university programs focused on enhancing human resources base space resource activities

In addition to the commercial interest, an emerging aspect of the space resources sector is the ongoing establishment of university and/or national institutes focused on training and development of space resources expertise. These include:

- *Colorado School of Mines Space Resources Graduate Program:* A global-first program focused on educating scientists, engineers, economists, entrepreneurs, and policy makers in the developing field of space resources, offers Post-baccalaureate Certificate and Master of Science (non-thesis) degree programs, as well as residential and online Ph.D. degree programs.

For Prospective Users of Capacity Building Programs	For Prospective Providers of Capacity Building Programs
1. Have you heard of capacity building? What does it mean to you?	1. What does capacity building mean to you?
2. What is the level of interest/exposure to space in your country? Does this subject matter to you/your people?	2. What are target audiences for a space-resources focused capacity building program? Why would those audiences be interested in such a program?
3. What is your experience with capacity building programs related to space technology or capabilities? In your experience what are the success factor and shortcomings of programs you have been involved in?	3. Could the existing capacity building programs you participate in, operate, or are aware of be adapted or revised to include topics related to space resources?
4. What level of involvement, participation, or awareness do you have of space resources (e.g. space mining or in-situ resource utilization) utilization or development?	4. What topics should be included in such a program?
5. In your region/area/sector – how do you view prospects for involvement in space resources utilization relation programs?	5. What are views on the prospects for implementation of capacity building programs related to space resources?

For Prospective Users of Capacity Building Programs	For Prospective Providers of Capacity Building Programs
6. Would a space resources focused capacity building program be useful to you?	
7. In your region/area/sector what are target audiences for a space-resources focused capacity building program? Why would those audiences be interested in such a program?	
8. Do you think that being part of (influencing decisions around) space resources' exploration, exploitation and knowledge is important? Why?	
9. Would you/your people like to have access to space resources and a seat at the discussion table on subjects related to space resources?	

- *The Luxembourg Interdisciplinary Space Master Program:* Partially funded by the Luxembourg Space Agency in connection to economic development of the space sector in Luxembourg, it is focused at providing 'participants from an engineering or scientific background with additional technical expertise in areas needed to support Luxembourg's space industry, along with a strong grounding in business.'
- *The proposed NASA Space Resources Institute:* The Space Resources Institute Act has been introduced in the U.S. Congress, which if passed would direct NASA to study the creation of the Space Resources Institute. The Institute would focus on enhancing and sponsoring basic scientific research and technology development related to space resources utilization

These programs might provide a basis of expertise which could be drawn into the foundations of international training programs focused on space resources capacity.

3 *Perspectives of Stakeholders*

Panel members conducted a *very limited* number of interviews done for context purposes – but not a significant or thorough sample. These interviews focused on emerging countries with no direct involvement in space resource activities. Topics raised in these interviews including lack of basic knowledge of space activities and the connection to daily lives/challenges; the need to make information accessible and relatable; concerns around making sure that diversity is truly well represented within the body(s) making decisions on space resource use; and desire to bridge the gap between haves and have-nots. It was also expressed that we could develop a stronger interest and exposure by reaching out to student populations, especially in science-focused disciplines.

Panel members have developed a number of recommended interview questions that might be used in future conversations to better understand the potential needs and features of capacity building activities focused on space resources:

4 *Suggestions for Space Resources Capacity Building Programs*

To achieve the benefit sharing models listed in Building Block 13, Panel members suggest that capacity building models need to consider two audiences/stakeholder groups: a) those who do not yet have access or an understanding about what is happening in the space resources sector and arena, and/or b) those who are aware, to a greater or lesser degree, on what is happening but are isolated by their decision-makers (sometimes even their peers). The overall goal of capacity building related space resources should be to facilitate access to, and exchange of, the knowledge and outcomes produced by space resource activities.

Space resources related capacity building programs can makes meaningful contributions as mechanisms/platforms that bring together those that have the knowledge and/or awareness of what is happening with those in the two stakeholder groups mentioned in the prior paragraph. An initial start to implementing this goal would be to identify a few topic areas (small number) that are of interest to both those that have the knowledge and those that could be introduced to capacity building activities or space-related programs that are open to international participation and in which participation can be primarily virtual. Discussion could initially start as a series of interview both types of participants in the mechanism/platform, those who have the knowledge to share and those who would receive it, asking them to identify their interest areas. Once a platform on an interest area gets establish, the discussions might be expected to develop into a real two-way exchange of information.

5 *Conclusion – Path Forward for Implementation of Space Resources Focused Capacity Building*

Two particular pathways to be considered in an implementation strategy for space resources focused capacity building activities include:

1. A curriculum model to be integrated into the Regional Centers for Space Science and Technology Education.
2. An ad-hoc working group – similar to WGCapD – to be instituted under an existing intergovernmental space exploration coordination body such as the International Space Exploration Coordination Group or the Lunar Exploration Analysis Group (LEAG) or Moon Village Association (MVA).

In suggesting such an implementation, the aim is to increase participation and engagement by those stakeholders whom are not directly involved in or access directly space resource activities. The aim is to facilitate access to, and exchange of, the knowledge and information produced by space resource activities. Capacity building in this concept does not necessarily imply direct participation in space resource activities, but rather the facilitation of awareness and education related to the sector and the ability to participate in indirect as well as direct manners (such as the utilization of scientific data collected through space resource activities). This could ultimately enhance the development of space sector expertise in the involved stakeholder states. As such there should be an awareness campaign as a part of capacity building. Awareness should not only focus on possible earthly benefits but also raise awareness of on-going initiatives and programs where scientist, technologists, economists, lawyers and other professionals from developing countries can participate.

Lastly it is important to note that as opposed to well-established research and user communities that have matured for decades, such as the EO community, the 'space resources' community is by and large limited to governmental programs, academic research institutions and a few companies that are willing to invest in a distant payoff. Identifying one or more communities that would have a stake or interest in exploring outer space and exploiting a variety of space resources would be of paramount importance to begin a capacity building process.

B Characterizing International Cooperation Models Related to Space Resources

1 *Introduction*

Throughout the Building Blocks the Working Group consistently references the value of, and calls for, international cooperation related to space resources utilization and in the development of frameworks to enable space resource activities. For example, Building Block 4 argues that 'international cooperation in space resource activities shall be conducted in accordance with international law' and Building Block 13 identifies several types of international cooperation that, if executed, might contribute to the sharing of benefits arising from space resources utilization. Furthermore, Building Block 1 suggests that any international framework on space resource activities should 'promote the identification of best practices by States, intergovernmental organizations, and non-governmental entities' – in the opinion of the Socio-Economic Panel, such best practices should include international cooperation models.

During the public commentary period on the draft Building Blocks the Working Group received a number of comments which suggested a need to provide further clarity and discussion of the role of international cooperation in the development of future framework for space resource activities. While it is not the role of the Working Group to suggest specific partnership models for States, it is in the interests of the community to better understand and characterize the methods, forms and models through which cooperation might be carried out, so that commonality and transparency in approach, intent, and objectives might be developed.

Significant work has been ongoing within UNCOPUOS (including its Legal Subcommittee) and other fora to describe cooperation models for space activities. This work provides an important basis of evidence for describing cooperation models related to space resources. UNCOPUOS has noted, in a Paper on Thematic Priority 1: Global Partnership in Space Exploration and Innovation,[1] that:

> 'in order to involve more countries in such international cooperation, there is a need to identify, during the sessions of the Committee on the Peaceful Uses of Outer Space, areas of common interest and to assign priorities for action to explore opportunities among the developers and users of space technologies.'

In order to apply this finding to space resources, and to provide further commentary on the international cooperation objectives included in the Building Blocks, the Socio-Economic Panel suggests in this whitepaper a method for standard characterization and discussion of space resources related international cooperation at the State and intergovernmental level. Postulating a five-group structure for classification of States based on capacity of government involvement/interest in space resources, each group is then described in terms of the models and objectives which might be employed by states at the level of capability for cooperation. This structure aims to document common objectives and cooperation models, and categorize them according to the states that are most likely to employ them. Following the development of the group structure a method is proposed for describing specific cooperation agreements in a common and standard way.

2 *Characterizing Cooperation Models for Space Resources*

In order to explore a wide range of possible cooperation models for the space resources segment, it is the Panel's understanding that the various groups of space actors (States, industry, academia) have different interests and objectives, which may vary according to their current human, social and financial capabilities. Spacefaring nations, space emerging

1 Thematic priority 1. Global partnership in space exploration and innovation, A/AC.105/C.1/114, 14 November 2017, par. 79.

nations and those with limited space capability may benefit from space resource activities in different ways. Section 2.a presents a suggestive characterization which served as a basis for further study of the topic.

a Groups: Actors' Capacity and Interest in Space Resources

In this Section, a brief characterization of groups is introduced. Note that due to actors' changing technological, scientific, and even social capabilities, their belonging to a particular group is fluid and may vary over time. Actors other than States are also included in this characterization.

GROUP 1 – Constituted by States (and/or their industries/institutions) that already possess technological capabilities, financial resources and interest in performing space resource activities.

GROUP 2 – Constituted by States (and/or their industries/institutions) with financial resources and capabilities, but no interest; or those with financial resources and interest, but no capabilities to perform space resource activities.

GROUP 3 – Constituted by States (and/or their industries/institutions) with little financial resources, little capacity and some space activity/space program.

GROUP 4 – Constituted by States (and/or their industries/institutions) with no financial resources, none or little capacity, very small or no space program. However, those States possess strategic minerals for space programs, e.g. niobium.

GROUP 5 – Constituted by States (and/or their industries/institutions) with no financial resources, none or little capacity, no space program, no strategic minerals.

b Matching Groups to Types of Relevant Cooperation Models

In this Section, the groups are combined with potential types of cooperation. Each group presented in the Section 2.a) can be described by specific types of cooperation. Such types were extracted from the UNCOPUOS Updated Draft Report of the Working Group on the Review of International Mechanisms for Cooperation in the Peaceful Exploration and Use of Outer Space.[2] The aim is to provide a better understanding of different approaches to cooperation in space activities taken by States and international organizations, as well as to identify types of cooperation relevant to space resource activities.

GROUP 1 – Public-Private Partnerships between public entities and International Industry, Bilateral R&D Agreements, Policy/Regulatory Coordination, Support of Capacity Building Programs, Industry to Industry Agreements.

GROUP 2 – Public-Private Partnerships between public entities and International Industry, Government-Government Agreement, Bilateral R&D Agreements. Intergovernmental

2 Updated Draft Report of the Working Group on the Review of International Mechanisms for Cooperation in the Peaceful Exploration and Use of Outer Space, A/AC.105/C.2/2017/CRP.27, 3 April 2017.

Agreement, Agency-Agency Memorandum of Understanding, Industry to Industry Agreements.

GROUP 3 – Government-Government Agreement, Bilateral R&D Agreements, Intergovernmental Agreement. Agency-Agency Memorandum of Understanding, Industry to Industry Agreements.

GROUP 4 – Government-Government Agreement, Bilateral R&D Agreements, Letter of Agreement, Letter of Intent, Industry to Industry Agreements.

GROUP 5 – Government-Government Agreement, Memorandum of Understanding, Letter of Agreement, Letter of Intent, Industry to Industry Agreements.

c Matching Groups to Objectives

This Section introduces a list of objectives of cooperation considering the groups' characterization, as in Section 2.a. It is important to note that objectives are group-related. For instance, 'social welfare improvement' might be an objective of cooperation for Group 5 with Group 1. It does not make much sense as a prime objective to those in Group 1.

Group 1	Public-Private Partnerships with:	Supporting government exploration programs
	International Industry	Reducing costs
	Bilateral R&D Agreements	Building industry capabilities
	Policy/Regulatory Coordination	Support domestic economic growth
	Support of Capacity Building Programs	Demonstrate/maintain leadership
	Industry to Industry	Legal mechanisms/instruments Building/consolidation
Group 2	Public-Private Partnerships with International Industry	Technology/capability development, capacity building, technical assistance, exchange of expertise
	Government-Government Agreement	Financial benefit from SR
	Bilateral R&D Agreements	Demonstrate space potential
	Intergovernmental Agreement	Observation of SR activity
	Agency-Agency MoU	
Group 3	Government-Government Agreement	Technology/capability development, capacity building
	Bilateral R&D Agreements	Mission minor participation
	Intergovernmental Agreement	Component testing, data sharing
	Agency-Agency MoU	Show some space potential
	Industry to Industry	

Group 4	Government-Government Agreement	Technology/capability development (from space to be applied on Earth)
	Bilateral R&D Agreements	Job creation from expertise acquired
	Letter of Agreement	Capacity building
	Letter of Intent	
	Industry to Industry	
Group 5	Government-Government Agreement	Access to funding arising from SR activities
	Memorandum of Understanding	Improvement of basic infrastructure
	Letter of Agreement	Social welfare improvement
	Letter of Intent	Capacity building
	Industry to Industry	

3 Conclusion: Describing the Variety of Cooperation Models for Space Resources

The Panel does not aim to propose ideal cooperation mechanisms or exhaustive list of available models. States will execute their sovereign freedom to select and determine participation in international cooperation following models that best suit their needs. However, having provided a suggested approach to characterizing the states involved as possible actors in space resources related cooperation, the possible forms of cooperation they might employ, and the possible objectives they might seek, the Panel concludes by providing a suggested approach to mapping and describing different cooperation models and objectives in a standard or common manner. Such an approach shows a richness and wide range of opportunities that relevant actors might explore and benefit from. It also promotes transparency and clarity in the discussion of space resources related cooperation while providing that state actors will choose the best model for cooperation depending on specific needs of the involved actors.

Such a mapping tool necessarily needs to include several factors including: 1) the actors involved in a cooperation and their level of capability/interest in space resources; 2) the objectives of cooperation; 3) the structure of the cooperation model; and 4) the topics of cooperation. In Section 2 of this whitepaper we have provided a description of actors, objectives, and structure. In this Section, we will show how those overall descriptive elements can be brought together into a common characterization of specific cooperation agreements.

The first step is to propose common language to describe the factors necessary to characterize agreements, drawing from the descriptive elements from Section 2 above. Table 1 suggests an approach for this.

Actor	Objective of Cooperation	Type / Form of Instrument	Topic of Cooperation *Topics to be highly specific to individual agreements. Example topics listed here:*
Group 1 (A1)	Supporting Government Exploration Programs (O1)	Govt-to-Govt Framework Agreement (T1)	Data sharing/access to data related to SR
Group 2 (A2)	Reducing Costs (O2)	Intergovernmental Agreement (T2)	Joint activity/project
Group 3 (A3)	Building Industry Capabilities (O3)	Agency to Agency MOUs (T3)	Technology sharing of SR
Group 4 (A4)	Support domestic economic growth (O4)	Implementing Arrangements (T4)	Capacity building in SR area
Group 5 (A5)	Demonstrate/maintain leadership (O5)	Letters of Agreement (T5)	Legal/policy issues
	Legal mechanisms/instruments building/consolidation (O6)	Letters of Intent (T6)	
	Solve legal issues and find fair arrangement regarding sharing responsibility and liability (O7)	Binding Bilateral	
	Open a dialogue and information exchange between cooperating states (O8)	Non-Binding Multilateral	
	Technology/capability development, capacity building, technical (09)	Regional	
	Etc.		

As an outcome of the performed analysis, the panel would suggest a case study using the factors identified to compile a specific characterization table that can be applied to describe specific cooperation agreements. The factors in Table 1 provide common terminology to describe cooperation models in a common way. Table 2 shows the structure of this proposed characterization table.

Agreement Between State A and State B

Actors (Objective)	Type/Form	*Topics:*
State A: A1 (O1, O3)	T1, Binding, Bilateral	*Example*
State B: A3 (O2)		

A next step in this analysis is to demonstrate the application of the characterization table to describe examples of current real-world cooperation agreements relating to space resources.

C Developing Responsible Finance Principles for Space Resources

1 *Introduction*

One of the most important elements to consider when thinking of the future space resources sector from the socio-economic perspective is a set of responsible investing principles. Taking from established principles in terrestrial sectors, the future space resources sector would be able to begin its activities on the right foot, avoiding various pitfalls from the start. A coherent, clear and accepted set of such principles will ensure a healthy operating environment for companies, with maximum possible acceptance of their activities back on Earth. Development and adherence to such a set of principles would contribute to the implementation of Building Block 10 – 'Avoidance of Harmful Impacts Resulting from Space Resources Activities' and Building Block 13 – 'Sharing of Benefits Arising from Space Resources Utilization' by instilling the belief, understanding, and implementation frameworks that these companies will be operating as responsible global citizens, something which is already now becoming critical for business on Earth.

In particular, corporations are supposed to be responsible not only for their impact of their own operations but also for the entire value chains such as processing and logistics for mining corporations. Finance, banking, and other industry sectors (including the terrestrial mining sector) have developed several sets of consensus principles to guide responsible investing, banking, and financing of terrestrial industry through impact on sustainable operations. In order to implement sustainability and ethics concepts into space resource management sector, the Socio-Economic Panel highly recommends considering and adapting such precedents to apply to space resources development. The targets for those who should adopt principles of this type – and be involved in their development – are focused on two groups: (1) space-resource development/utilization companies (and their primary customer groups) and (2) investors, lenders, and credit providers for those companies.

2 *Review of the Existing Principles*

Our recommendation to develop these principles originates from existing de-facto sustainable business governance for important sectors such as mining, energy, food and agriculture, chemicals and clothing. For the past decade, investors embarked on integrating ESG (Environmental, Social and Governance) issues into their asset investment decision-making from the perspective of both long-term financial performance and ethics. ESG integration started from public equity investment, and has since expanded to cover private equity and fixed income investing. Specifically, in the terrestrial mining sector, the Sustainability Accounting Standards Board has developed the Sustainability Accounting Standard (SASB Standard) for Metals & Mining and the International Finance Corporation (IFC) has published a guide for sustainable and responsible mining.

Further examples of these self-regulatory principles include:

- *UN Principles of Responsible Investment (PRI)*: a set of principles to consider 'investment implications of environmental, social and governance (ESG) factors' and to support implementation through enabling an 'international network of investor signatories in incorporating these factors into their investment and ownership decisions.'[3]
- *UN Principles for Responsible Banking (PRB)*: a set of principles designed to 'framework for the sustainable banking system of the future, and help the industry to demonstrate how it makes a positive contribution to society.'[4]
- *Equator Principles*: a 'risk management framework, adopted by financial institutions, for determining, assessing and managing environmental and social risk in projects. It is primarily intended to provide a minimum standard for due diligence and monitoring to support responsible risk decision-making.'[5]
- *OECD Guidelines for Multinational Enterprise*: a set of 'recommendations from governments to multinational enterprises on responsible business conduct. The OECD Guidelines set standards for responsible business conduct across a range of issues such as human rights, labor rights, and the environment.'[6]
- *ISO 26000*: an 'international standard developed to help organizations effectively assess and address social responsibilities that are relevant and significant to their mission and vision; operations and processes; customers, employees, communities, and other stakeholders; and environmental impact.'

Of these, PRI and PRB, are most instructive in thinking about the space resources investment. A reference list for these, and others, is included at the end of this paper.

3 *See* https://www.unpri.org/pri (accessed and verified on 20 December 2019).
4 *See* https://www.unepfi.org/banking/bankingprinciples/ (accessed and verified on 20 December 2019).
5 *See* https://equator-principles.com (accessed and verified on 20 December 2019).
6 *See* https://www.oecdwatch.org/oecd-ncps/the-oecd-guidelines-for-mnes/ (accessed and verified on 20 December 2019).

3 Applying Existing Practice to Space Resources Development

ESG (Environmental, Social and Governance) issues can be integrated in company practice for space resources utilization through both the investor and corporate/firm channels. At this early stage in the development of a space resources sector, development of guidelines and principles for investing are likely to be more fruitful than development of industry standards – as the industry community is small, technical and operations practices are not developed, and revenue streams have not been secured, standards would likely be premature. However, investment and finance sources – in consultation and cooperation with the space resources business sector – can provide positive influence on industry practice. This is also in keeping with the Hague Group's principle of adaptive governance.

a For Investors and Financiers – Application of PRI and PRB

PRI and PRB are intended to provide international best practice which financers could use to align investment decision frameworks with ESG integration. ESG principles can be aligned with multiple stages of the investing decision, to help ensure that investments are made in companies that will follow responsible ESG practice. The following chart outlines the application to phases of a private-equity investment (loan providers may also adopt a similar framework:

Pre-financing	During Financing	End of Deal
Screening	***Engagement***	***Exit***
–Compile a checklist to screen for high-level ESG risks	–Develop an active ownership policy including engagement and proxy voting	–Define standards to make an exit to a 'right' new investor
–Establish an exclusion list for high-level checks	–Collaborate with financed company to set up an ESG program	
–Consider ESG factor during detailed company due diligence	–Leverage financed company board to implement ESG initiatives	
Investment Decision	***Monitoring***	
–Include ESG considerations as standard practice in investment committee discussions	–Define company specific ESG indicators	
–Include ESG findings from due diligence in the investment memorandum	–Prioritize ESG issues and focus on the most important issues in the short/medium term	
Investment Agreement	–Require financed companies to make action plans on important social and environmental issues and disclose them to the public	

Pre-financing	During Financing	End of Deal
-Share ESG objectives, policies and practices with financed company	-Ensure compliance with relevant flag country laws, regulations and permits that pertain to environmental and social issues	
-Seek formal commitment from financed company by incorporating ESG issues into the deal documents	-Ensure ESG considerations are consistently on the financed company's board agenda	
-Formulate a roadmap with a defined time horizon with clear process benchmarks	-Collect information on ESG developments from financed company and include in annual review	
	-Monitor ESG developments in internal review meetings	

b For Space Resources Companies and Customers – SASB Standards Like Product for Space Resources

As the space resources industry matures – early integration of ESG principles through the investment culture could be leveraged to develop industry voluntary consensus standards for responsible conduct. These standards might be modeled after or develop based upon content in the existing SASB Standard for Metals & Mining. The might also incorporate elements being developed specifically for space resources – such as the 'safety zones' being considered by the Technical Panel. The following chart identifies elements of the SASB Standard for Metals & Mining that might be relevant or applicable to space resource activities (Table 3).

Theme	Operations in Celestial Bodies	Delivery to the Earth
GHG Emissions		X
Air Quality		X
Energy Management	X	
Water Management	X	
Waste & Hazardous Materials Management	X	X
Biodiversity Principles	X	X
Security, Human Rights, and Rights of Indigenous Peoples		
Workforce Health, Safety, and Well-being	X	
Prevention of Corruption	X	X

Given the early and speculative status of the space resources industry, and the Hague Working Group's principle of adaptive governance, setting operational standards is difficult to foresee at this stage, due to the amount of unknowns in many operational areas. Thus, initially such standards would likely focus on disclosure and transparency of activities

4 Conclusion: Path Forward for Development of Space Resources Investment Principles

We recommend that, as an implementation action following the finalization of the Building Blocks, a separate set of principles be created specifically for Responsible Investment in Space Resources. These principles would draw from the existing practice in the banking, finance, and terrestrial mining sectors (e.g. the references provided in this paper), would have a unique set of features specific to space resources circumstances, and could potentially serve as an informing factor for the future development of industry operator focused best practices and/or standards – once the space resources industry matures to a point in which these become relevant.

In many ways the process for developing these Principles for Responsible Investment in Space Resources might look similar to the process through which The Hague International Space Resources Governance Working Group operated. A set of draft and/or recommend principles would be drafted by a civil society group of investors (including banks and private equity); space resources entrepreneurs & customers; policy and regulatory experts; and representatives who were involved in the development of the existing PRI & PRB documents. The process would also need to consider relationship of the Principles to other initiatives to encourage or measure responsible space activities – including standards products and activities like the forthcoming Space Sustainability Rating being developed by the World Economic Forum and its partners. Once recommended Principles are developed, they will would be passed to international bodies for formal review and official implementation as accepted industry standards.

Selected Reference List

Equator Principles (2013). Equator Principles III. Available from http://equator-principles.com/wp-content/uploads/2017/03/equator_principles_III.pdf.

PRI (2011). A Practical Guide to Active Ownership in Listed Equity. Retrieved on 20 December 2019 from https://www.unpri.org/download?ac=4151.

PRI (2014). Integrating ESG in Private Equity: A Guide for General Partners. Retrieved on 20 December 2019 from https://www.unpri.org/download?ac=252.

PRI (2018). Responsible Investment in Private Equity: A Guide for Limited Partners (2nd ed.). Retrieved on 20 December 2019 from https://www.unpri.org/download?ac=260.

PRB (2019). Principles for Responsible Banking. Retrieved on 20 December 2019 from https://www.unepfi.org/banking/bankingprinciples/.

D Applying Social License to Operate to Space Resources

This group of Socio-Economic Panel members feels that issues around Social License to Operate (SLO) are important for space resource firms and governments to consider to ensure orderly and productive activity in space. To be clear, SLO is given to firms by stakeholders when actions are taken that go beyond regulatory compliance with applicable laws. Obviously, nothing tangible or legal is taken away but issues like people blocking entrance to a site or customers refusing to buy something is what ultimately occurs. This white paper outlines what SLO is, gives a couple of case studies that we feel are relevant to space resources, and discusses common themes when considering whether stakeholders will provide a SLO.

1 Introduction

As space resources utilization, development, and commercialization develops into a functional market over the next decades, it raises questions both of the potential benefit and impact to both emerging space-capable states (whom might not have the industrial capacity to directly participate in commercial space resource activities); and of possible disruption to terrestrial extractive industries (and the stakeholders that relate to those industries). Both of these points raised affect stakeholder groups, who while perhaps not directly participating in the initial development of space resources utilization, have an interest in the outcomes. While specific benefits and impacts to these stakeholder interests may not be easily identifiable at this stage of development, under the principle of adaptive governance, several Building Blocks relate to these questions, most notably Building Block 13 and Building Block 9.

This whitepaper explores the relationship of a concept used in the terrestrial extractive industry – Social License to Operate (SLO) – to space resources utilization. The term Social License to Operate (SLO) generally refers to efforts and activities an extractive company takes to building and maintain goodwill or social capital with the communities near where they operate. This goodwill is generated by activities to ensure the affected community benefits (monetarily or non-monetarily) as a result of the extractive operations. SLO can also address efforts to mitigate harmful or negative impacts of operations. It is important to note that SLO activities are above and beyond what is legally required for a firm to operate. As such common elements addressed through SLO activities can help to identify and described both commons types of benefits arising from extractive activities and the ways in which operators interact with stakeholder to address negative impacts.

In particular, applying SLO to space resource activities may help develop a implementation context under Building Block 9, which states the 'international framework should provide that States and intergovernmental organizations authorizing space resource activities shall give due regard to the interests of all countries and humankind.' While 'due regard' has a legal dimension (which we will not attempt to address in this paper); it also has policy and market interaction aspects. SLO may be instructive as an example of how terrestrial extractive industry operators give due regard to the interests of the stakeholders affected by their operations.

2 *What Is Social License to Operate*

In this section, we explain how SLO are either taken away from a firm or how firms act in order to maintain their SLO. As these cases establish, stakeholders may attempt to take away a firm's SLO even if they are not directly extracting or purchasing the product. We hope these case study examples provide concrete examples of how a firm (and by default government authorizing the actions of the firm) can show due regard for stakeholders by the firms' actions.

2.1 Case Example One: Pakistani Fertilizer – Illustrating how SLO is Given between Parties Directly Linked with an Economic Activity and how a Party Can Revoke its SLO and Create Disruptions

The fertilizer industry (mainly urea manufacturing) in Pakistan is mostly located in one main area (Northern Sindh) which is close to a major gas field – Mari field. The population in the region is mostly rural and constitutes mainly low-income farmers with small urban centers. The industry draws on the local rural population for its unskilled labor. Even though these fertilizer plants are the main source of economic activity in the region, at times the workers carry out protests and strikes. These strikes mainly happen as a negotiating tool during the periodic union contract negotiations and at times to get the fertilizer industry or a specific player to meet certain one-off demands or due to some incidents. This leads to serious disruptions in plant operations and economic loss for the fertilizer industry.

This is an example of a stakeholder revoking a firm's SLO. Here the rural population through employment in the fertilizer industry exercise its SLO. The benefit to the local populations translates through the employment and the economic activity generated from the presence of the industry. However, when the local population feels that the benefits from the fertilizer industry are not fairly accruing to the local population, they revoke the SLO provided to the fertilizers industry through protests or strikes.

This SLO instance can apply to the space resources example to demonstrate the relationship between the developing and developed countries. Like the Pakistani fertilizer industry example, a relatively weaker party such as developing countries can exert power and control over the stronger party country/firm carrying out space resources related activity.

The power/influence can from control over a strategic or essential input required for an economic activity. As an example of power or control can be launch/landing pad locations. Due to economic benefits it may be cheaper to launch from equator or near to the equator and most of the countries lying at the equator are developing countries. Therefore, these countries can exert some influence and control over the space mining activity and may disrupt these activities.

The basic idea of SLO related to the guiding principle that space will benefit all humankind. As underdeveloped countries may not be able to undertake these ventures (due to funding constraints or technology issues) they will be missing out on the benefits from the spaces resources and if they can exert some influence or control directly on the space resource activities, they may do so as shown in the above case.

2.2 Case Example Two: Apple Cobalt Mining – Illustrating how Relatively Different Economic Activities Can Be Linked and how an SLO can be Provided by Different or Unrelated Actors/Players in the Market

Apple is considered one of the largest cell-phone manufactures in the world with its iconic smart series – iPhone. Cobalt is a main raw material for lithium-ion batteries used in smart phones such as iPhone. More than half of the supply of cobalt comes from mines in Democratic Republic of Congo (DRC).

As per an Amnesty International report released in 2016 most of the mines in DRC use child labor as young as 7 years of age working in hazardous and inhumane conditions. Although iPhone is not directly responsible for the mining of cobalt but being the end user of the mineral, Apple faced a lot of pressure from human rights group and eventually its customers to address the issue of the working conditions of cobalt miners. In order to avoid media and economic backlash, Apple took various steps to address its supply chain issues and tried to ensure responsible sourcing of its minerals.

This above example demonstrates how two relatively different activities in a supply chain can be linked together and create issues for a company down the supply chain. Here

Apple was in danger of losing its SLO which was given by the customers and the world at large through various human rights organizations. In the case of space resource activities, although economic activities will be carried in outer space, there is a possibility that the countries/stakeholder here provide the SLO to the country/firm carrying out these activities. Therefore, there is a need to be cognizant of the impact of these activities on seemingly unrelated players. It also demonstrates the ability of companies to react to and revise activities in light of concerns from consumer stakeholders.

3 *Typical or Common Themes/Issues Addressed in SLO Practices*

There are many issues that trigger or lead to discussions of removing a firm's SLO. This section will discuss a couple of these issues in detail but the discussion is not meant to be comprehensive. One common theme in many SLO issues is a feeling of inequality or unfairness from some stakeholders, which leads to the potential or attempted removal of a firm's SLO. This group is happy to provide additional material on common themes should the Working Group find that useful.

3.1 Common SLO Topics

3.1.1 Indigenous Peoples/Standing Rock

Following Article I of the Outer Space Treaty, 'the exploration and use of outer space (...) shall be carried out for the benefit and in the interests of all countries (...) and shall be the province of all mankind,' we deduce that any group on Earth may potentially exercise SLO rights in outer space, specifically in terms of cultural heritage and environmental preservation. These groups include indigenous communities.

Several controversies on Earth involving indigenous groups exercising their SLOs in mining and pipeline building operations have revealed that redistribution of economic benefits alone is not enough to find negotiated solutions. In the case of the Standing Rock Dakota Pipeline protests of 2016, for instance, indigenous groups and their supporters put forward environmental, cultural, and spiritual arguments to stop the building of the pipeline, namely, that construction under Lake Oahe and other nearby water bodies threatened not only the community's water supply but also ancient burial grounds that are fundamental for their culture to persist. Resistance against the shrinking of Grand Staircase-Escalante National Monument in Utah based upon heritage and conservation claims is also representative of culturally-motivated exercises of SLOs.

3.1.2 Environmental Impacts

Environmental concerns may also influence the approval and maintenance of a company's SLO. In order to gain and keep its SLO, a company must be able to meet its stakeholders' expectations regarding its environmental footprint (Richert et al., 2015). Particularly, there is already a growing amount of academic literature that studies the environmental impacts of various domains of the space industry. The European Space Agency's Clean Space initiative (ESA Clean Space, 2019) is developing a common framework to guide the environmental impact assessment of the European space sector's projects and programs. The environmental impact categories of this framework include climate change, stratospheric ozone depletion, resources depletion (including water and land use), human and environmental toxicity, and acidification. Life Cycle Assessment has been proposed as the most appropriate tool to quantify, integrate, and evaluate the performance of a space project across these categories throughout its life cycle, from initial design to production and assembly, to utilization, and, finally, to disposal after the end-of-life. Some of the most complete studies that have been conducted to this end (Maury et al., 2017) investigated the environmental impacts of launchers (production and assembly, launch campaign, and launch event), of whole missions (launchers, satellite, and ground support activities), and of different space propellants (manufacturing processes, and relevant space materials).

This past work will prove useful to aspiring space resources companies, in order for them to preemptively avoid detrimental impacts to both the global and the local environment. This is especially true in the proximity of launching sites and falling regions of discarded launch vehicle stages (Koroleva et al., 2018), where it is likely that the majority of the abovementioned noxious impacts will be most intensely manifested. Thus, the incorporation of the Environmental Impacts theme in SLO practice could mitigate the emergence of local opposition that might arise due to a perceived imbalance in environmental equity, as was the case with a recently proposed commercial spaceport on an ecologically significant site in Hawaii (Weatherboy.com, 2019). In addition to the detrimental impacts on the terrestrial environment, if Mars becomes an interesting target for outbound space resources missions, the impact of the biological contamination on the planet's environment due to improper microbial bioburden reduction of the relevant equipment should also be assessed. This is in line with COSPAR's Planetary Protection Policy (Kminek et al., 2017), since it could cause harmful interference with the state of the in situ available resources, such as any potential subsurface aquifers (Rummel, 2016).

3.2 Summary

There are a couple of lessons for the Working Group to consider as they continue their work. First, space resource firms and the governments who support them cannot be assured of having a SLO just by following all regulatory requirements. SLO is maintained through firms treating all aspects of their supply chain in a way that is considered fair by most of the stakeholders. Second, actions taken by firms to maintain their SLO do not have to be purely monetary. There are many aspects of SLO practices that lead to lower overall costs to the firm (and potentially higher revenues to the government). Finally, a firm does not have to be directly extracting the resource or the first entity downstream (first person to purchase from the extractive firm) to be impacted by SLO concerns or have their SLO revoked.

4 Conclusion: Applying SLO to Space Resources

As space resource activities mature, SLO provides a helpful tool to help anticipate challenges to space resources operations. We must remember, however, that legal/economic premises alone may be insufficient to address resistance based upon sociocultural, heritage and preservation, as well as environmental claims. Considering the SLO of space resources provides a conceptual framework through which different stakeholder groups potentially affected by space resource activities can interact in a discussion with the space resources sector. Certain examples have been given in this paper to the define the concept of SLO and its and relevance to space resources; further work could be conducted to briefly explore and related SLO to the implementation of a number of Building Blocks including: 4.2, 4.3, 9, 10, 12, 13, 16.2, 18.

References

ESA Clean Space (2019). ESA Clean Space – Ecodesign. [Online] Retrieved on 20 December 2019 from https://www.esa.int/Safety_Security/Clean_Space/ecodesign.

Kminek, G., Conley, C., Hipkin, V. & Yano, H. (2017). COSPAR's Planetary Protection Policy. Paris: COSPAR.

Koroleva, T. V. et al. (2018). The environmental impact of space transport. *Transportation Research Part D: Transport and Environment*, Vol. 58, pp. 54-69.

Maury, T. et al. (2017). How to Integrate Space Debris Issue into the Environmental Assessment of Space Missions. Darmstadt, Germany, 7th European Conference on Space Debris, 18-21 April 2017.

Richert, C., Rogers, A. & Burton, M. (2015). Measuring the extent of a Social License to Operate: The influence of marine biodiversity offsets in the oil and gas sector in Western Australia. *Resources Policy*, Vol. 43, pp. 121-129.

Rummel, J. D. (2016). Planetary protection for human missions: Options and implications. Big Sky, MT, USA, Aerospace Conference, 2016 IEEE. 5-12 March 2016.

Weatherboy.com (2019). Spaceport Plans Launched with Sparks in Hawaii. [Online]. Retrieved on 20 December 2019 from www.weatherboy.com/spaceport-plans-launched-sparks-hawaii/.

'This Is What We Die For' – Human Rights Abuses in The Democratic Republic of the Congo Power The Global Trade In Cobalt. Retrieved on 20 December 2019 from https://www.amnesty.org/download/Documents/AFR6231832016ENGLISH.PDF.